capturemychicago™

Presented by

Sponsored by

Foreword

What does Chicago look like to you?

The answer is contained inside the pages of this book—and on the DVD that comes with it.

The answer is found in the serenity of a sunrise over Lake Michigan, the strength of our architecture, the beauty of our parks and neighborhoods, and the spirit of all Chicagoans.

This was a simple idea. We asked you to send us your pictures of what it is like to live in Chicagoland and vote for your favorite photos. The result is this beautiful book—an enduring and powerful snapshot of our lives, created by the collective vision of the people.

We would like to thank everybody who cast nearly 2.4 million votes and submitted more than 28,000 photos.

We believe that we have indeed captured Chicago. We hope you agree. Go ahead, turn the pages and enjoy. You just might see Chicago like you never have before.

The staff of CBS 2

Table of Contents

 FRIENDLY FACES 4
 SCAPES OF ALL SORTS 34
 LANDMARKS & ARCHITECTURE 94
 SPORTS SPIRIT 16
 NEWSWORTHY 82
 RECREATION & CELEBRATION 128
 ARTS, CULTURE & FOOD 24
 PETS 68

PRIZE WINNERS 152
PHOTOGRAPHER DIRECTORY 153
SPONSOR 160

About this book.

Capture My Chicago™ is all about how you see the Greater Chicago area. It started with a simple idea: Lots of folks take lots of pictures of the Chicago area, many of which would be worthy of publishing in a fine-art, coffee-table book. Knowing that thousands of photos would be submitted, we posed the question: How do we pick the best from the rest?

The answer was genius. We put the editing power in the hands of the people. Local people. People who know Chicago. People just like you. We asked photographers, doctors, union workers, musicians, moms, right-handed people, pants-wearing folks, or anyone from any walk of life to vote for what they considered to be the photos that best capture the Chicago area.

From 28,144 photo submissions to the pages of this book, 2,388,443 votes helped shape what you hold in your hands. It's something that's never been done before: publishing by vote. Enjoy it.

How to use this book.

Open. Look at the best pictures you've ever seen. Repeat. Actually, maybe there's a little more to it. First, be sure to check out the prize winners in the back of the book (also marked with ★ throughout). You'll also want to watch the DVD. It's got more than a thousand photos on it! Here's the caption style so you can be sure to understand what's going on in each photo:

PHOTO TITLE *(position on page)*
Location photo taken, if available
Caption, mostly verbatim as submitted. 📷 **PHOTOGRAPHER**

Copyright info.

Copyright © 2009 • ISBN: 978-1-59725-232-4 | All rights reserved. No part of this book may be reproduced, stored in a retrieval system or transmitted in any form or by any means, electronic, mechanical, photocopying, recording or otherwise, without prior written permission of the copyright owner or the publisher. All photographers retain full rights of their photos that appear in this publication.

Do not use or copy any images from this book without written permission from the photographer. Note: photos may appear in different chapters than they were submitted. Prize awards were not affected. For more information on the Capture My Chicago Web site, please contact Pediment Publishing (books@pediment.com). Published by Pediment Publishing, a division of The Pediment Group, Inc. www.pediment.com. Printed in Canada. CAPTURE and Capture My Chicago are trademarks of The Pediment Group, Inc.

Friendly Faces

BUCKTOWN SPIRIT (left)
Bucktown Neighborhood
Enjoying the warm weather, Tony Gilbert Davis (left) and Shaina Hoffman sit on a ledge outside their apartment in Wicker Park near North Ave. on December 30, 2008. They said it wasn't the first time they have done this!
📷 AL PODGORSKI

MAN FEEDING PIGEONS (bottom left)
A man feeds pigeons some crumbled pizza crust on the steps of the Cultural Center.
📷 JOHN MALOOF

HEHE (bottom middle)
Northwest Side
My niece on her tricycle down a typical Chicago neighborhood block. 📷 MARICEL CRUZ

UNTITLED (bottom right)
Happy little girl. 📷 JANESSA BULLEN

GOOGLY EYES! (above)
Naperville
This makes me laugh! 📷 **JONATHAN ROBSON**

MARIE *(above)*
Palatine, IL
A wide-angle perspective of a bright smiling face. 📷 **DAVID APRIL**

C'MON GET HAPPY! *(above)*
Bristol Renaissance Faire, Bristol, WI
You know you are depressed when an elephant tries to cheer you up. 📷 **BETH BROUSIL**

MUD PLAY *(above)*
Cortland Street, Bucktown
Summer neighborhood fun in the mud.
📷 **RYAN ZOGHLIN**

★ **WONDERING EYES** *(above)*
Cermak Ave., Chicago
A portrait taken right off of Cermak.
📷 **CLIFTON HENRI**

I WANT YOU! *(previous left)*
Dank Haus, Chicago
I shot this at a wedding recently. This is one of many congratulatory portraits I made that evening. 📷 **CAREY PRIMEAU**

FROZEN BEAUTY *(previous right)*
Madison Street, Forest Park, Illinois
During a break in a typical Chicago snow storm, I asked this young lady if she would pose for a photograph. She did, and this is the result. Who would have ever thought the snow could be so beautiful! 📷 **SAMUEL BARR**

★ WAITING ON THE TRAIN *(above)*
Red Line State and Lake
Big sister takes little brother home from school.
📷 MIKE OOLEMAN

FATHER/SON *(right top)*
Greg shares a moment with his son, three-month-old Brewer in their Frankfort, Illinois backyard. 📷 JEAN LACHAT

UNTITLED *(right bottom)*
Jazz legend Koko Taylor belts out a tune at a benefit concert at the Riviera Theatre.
📷 MICHAEL BRACEY

Obama
Our next president

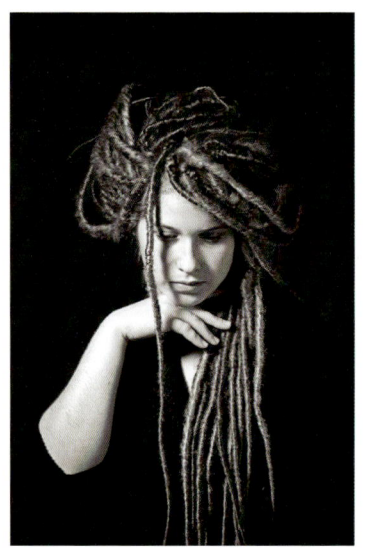

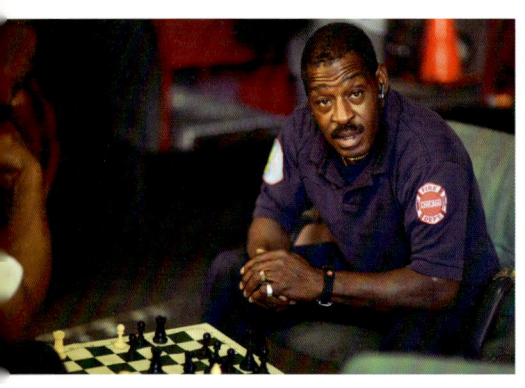

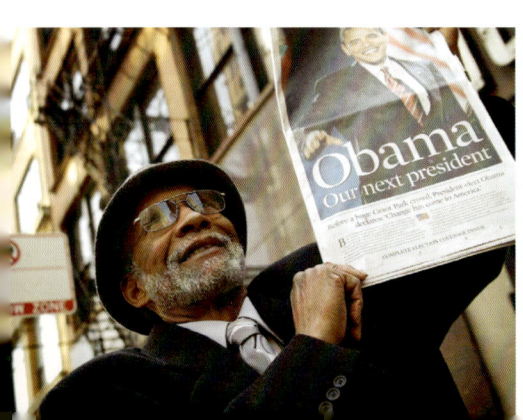

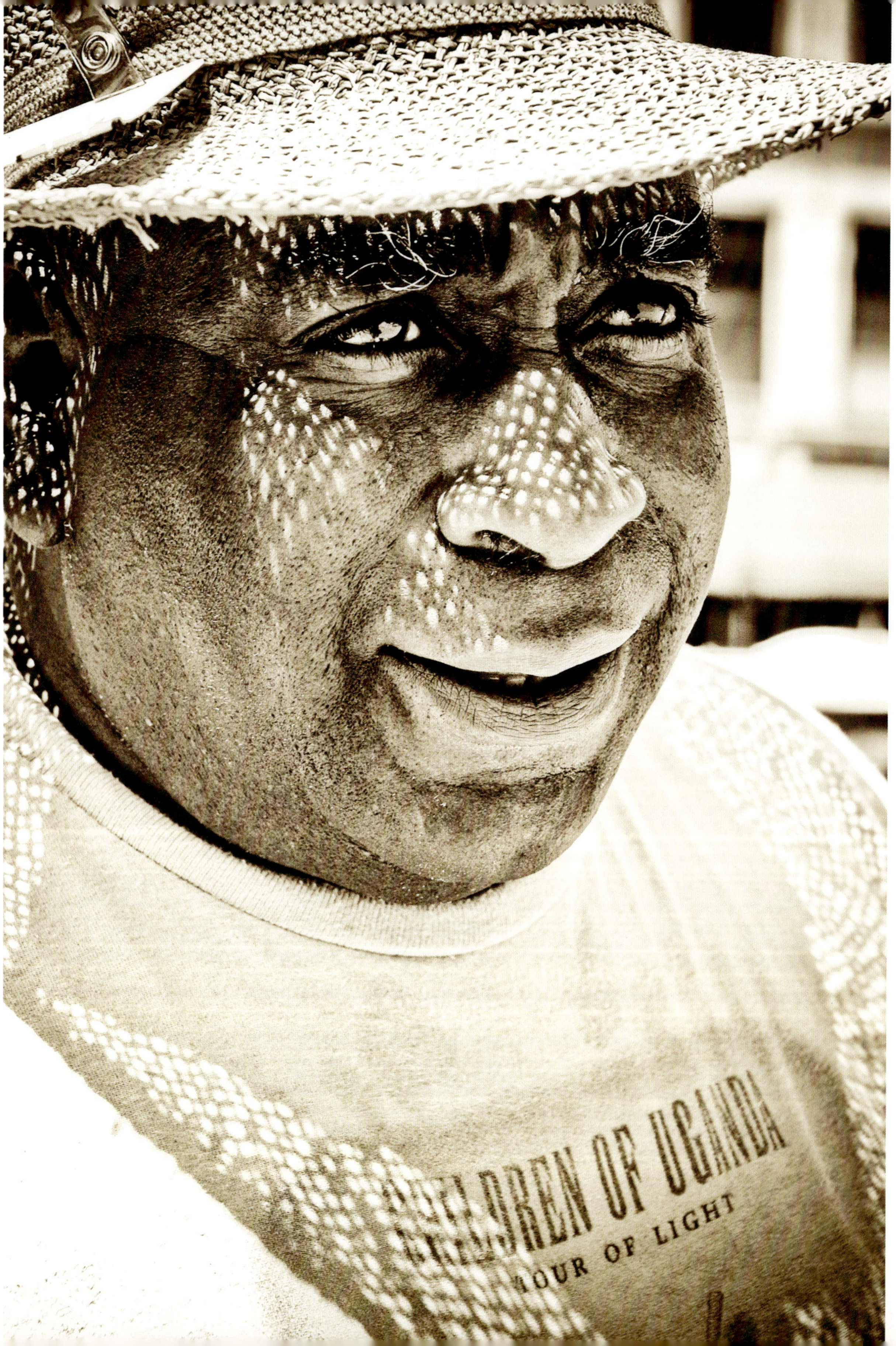
OF UGANDA
OF LIGHT

> "I don't remember his name, but his smile will stick with me forever."
> — CHRISTOPHER WILSON/UNTITLED

UNTITLED *(left)*
Ebenezer Lutheran Church, Chicago
A distinguished gentleman with a great smile who I ran into at a church function. 📷 **CHRISTOPHER WILSON**

ALICJA *(opposite top)*
Alicja came to school one day with these gorgeous dreadlocks. I knew at that moment that I had to capture her newest defining characteristic on film. 📷 **JENNIFER JACKSON**

CFD *(opposite middle)*
Chicago
A very friendly face when you need him! 📷 **JONATHAN ROBSON**

IN MY LIFETIME *(opposite bottom)*
Wabash and VanBuren, Downtown Chicago
My 75-year-old grandfather in one of his proudest moments.
📷 **CLIFTON HENRI**

MR. DRUMMER (MR. ROBINSON) *(opposite right)*
Michigan Ave. at Millennium Park
Back in 2005, this gentleman, a drumming street performer, allowed me to take his photo. The shot sat around on my hard drive for two years before I posted it. It was color and not exactly all that interesting. After a sepia treatment, it became one of my favorite street portraits.
📷 **CHRISTOPHER WILSON**

NEIGHBORS (left)
Devon and Talman
In most other places in the world, these two would seem worlds apart. Here, in West Rogers Park, however, they are neighbors who shop at the same grocery store, walk the same streets, take the same buses and enjoy the warmth of the same sun. 📷 **SARAH RHEE**

PROUD GRANDMA (opposite top)
Millennium Park
Photographing the photographer at the Crown Fountain. 📷 **KEN ILIO**

BELLA (opposite bottom)
O'Hare Airport
Bella Hendry, 5, frustrated at O'Hare International Airport while moving to another terminal. Bella, her sister, and mom were flying standby and were at the airport all day. 📷 **TAMARA BELL**

SMITHE (opposite right)
A portrait of a friend I met on the street.
📷 **BRIAN HAGY**

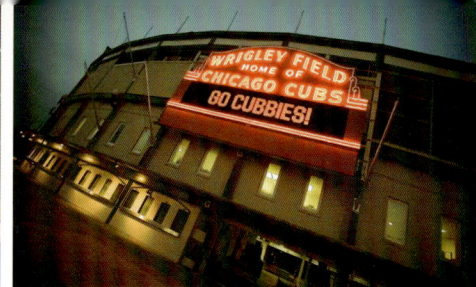

Sports Spirit

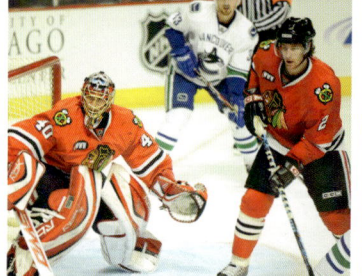

COACH DON (top)
Coach Don gets a signed ball from his Rays team following the end of their season in Mokena, Illinois. The team took second place in their division. JEAN LACHAT

HELMET AND FIELD (bottom left)
Naperville, Illinois
The inaugural year of Metea Valley High School football. LAURENCE PEARLMAN

★ **CATCHER** (bottom right)
Jessie, 7, steps in as catcher during a game in Mokena, Illinois. JEAN LACHAT

★ **ANOTHER END TO A DISAPPOINTING SEASON** (following left)
With the Cubs not looking to make the playoffs, empty seats mark another season of dashed hopes. ERWIN ARAOS

SUMMER SOLSTICE SUNSET AT WRIGLEY FIELD (following top left)
Sunset at the field of our dreams.
GEOFF HALLIDAY

WRIGLEY FIELD NIGHT (following top right)
An evening baseball game at Wrigley Field in May 2005 against the New York Mets.
JOHN CROUCH

GREAT NIGHT FOR A BALLGAME (following bottom)
A great night for a ballgame. Awesome weather on a feel-good night. Chicago White Sox vs. Kansas City, August, 2009. White Sox lost 5-4. Think positive, they will win.
MARGARET WALSH

WRIGLEY FIELD
HOME OF
CHICAGO CUBS
WELCOME TO
WRIGLEY FIELD

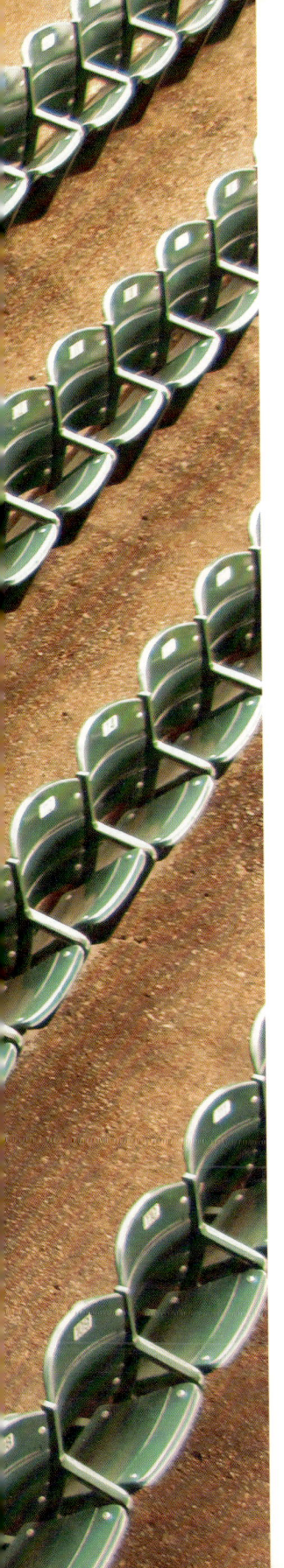

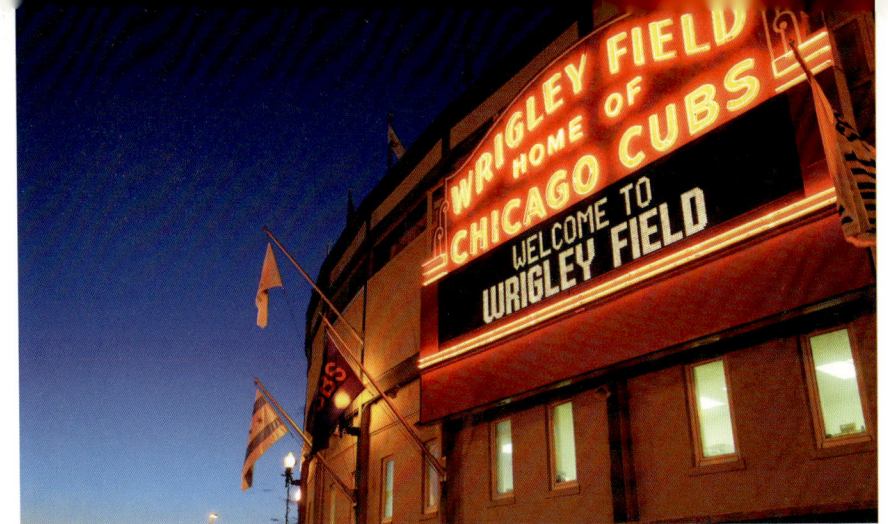

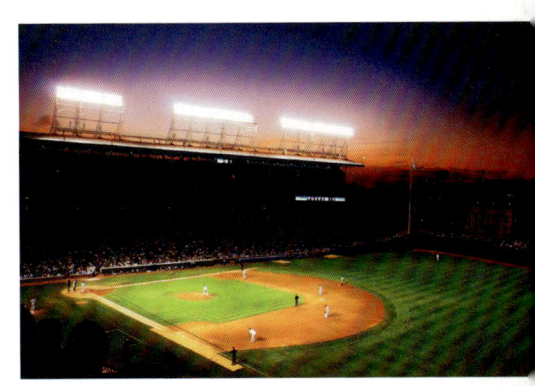

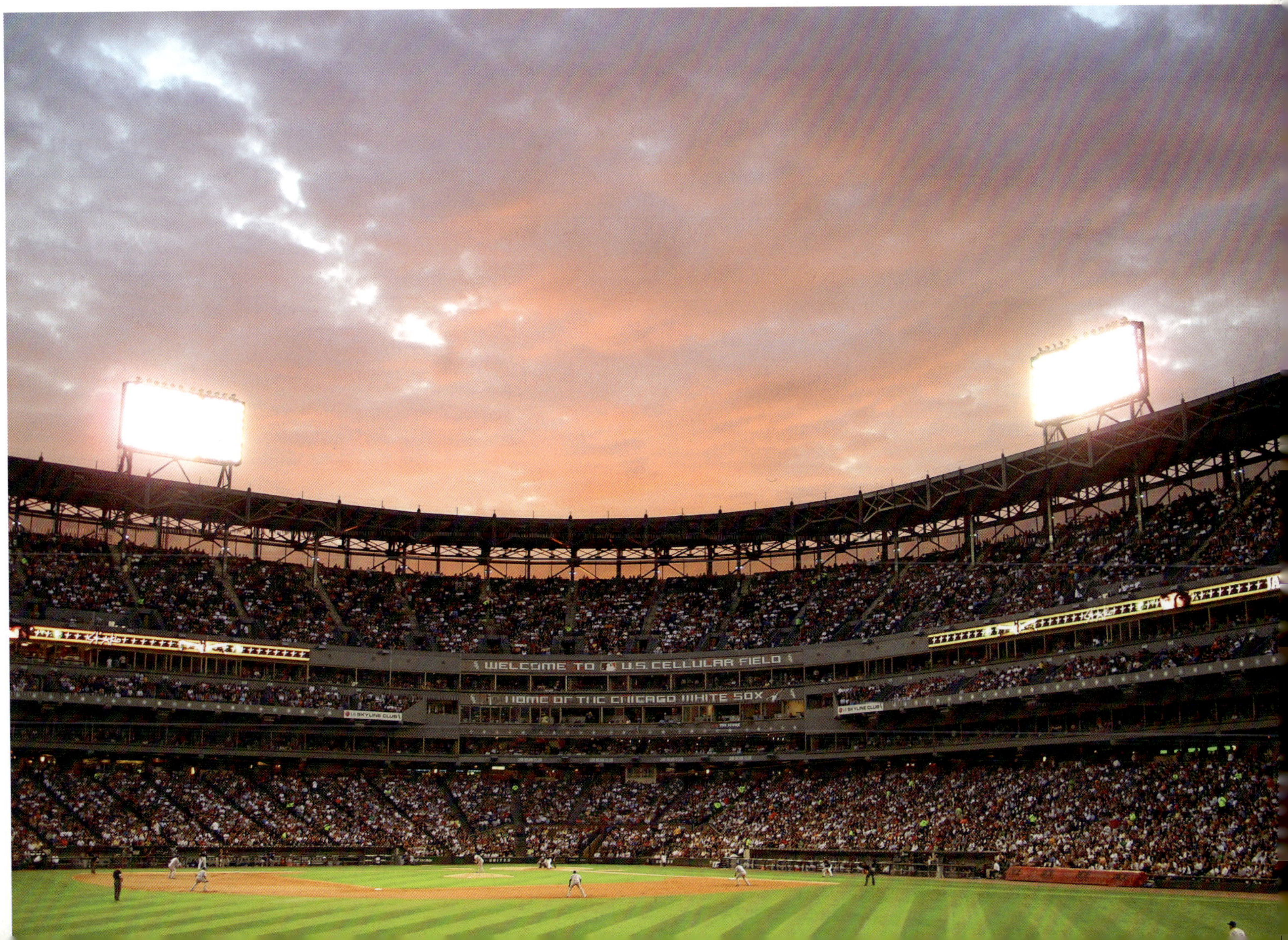
WELCOME TO U.S. CELLULAR FIELD
HOME OF THE CHICAGO WHITE SOX

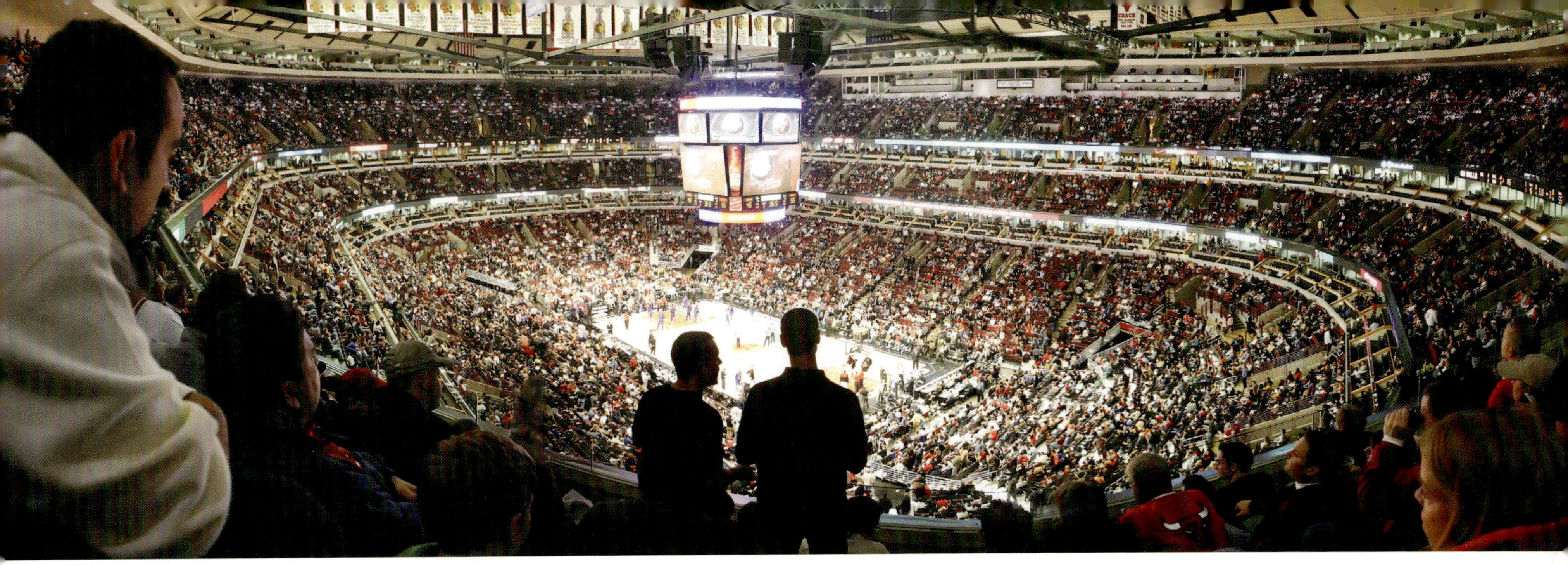

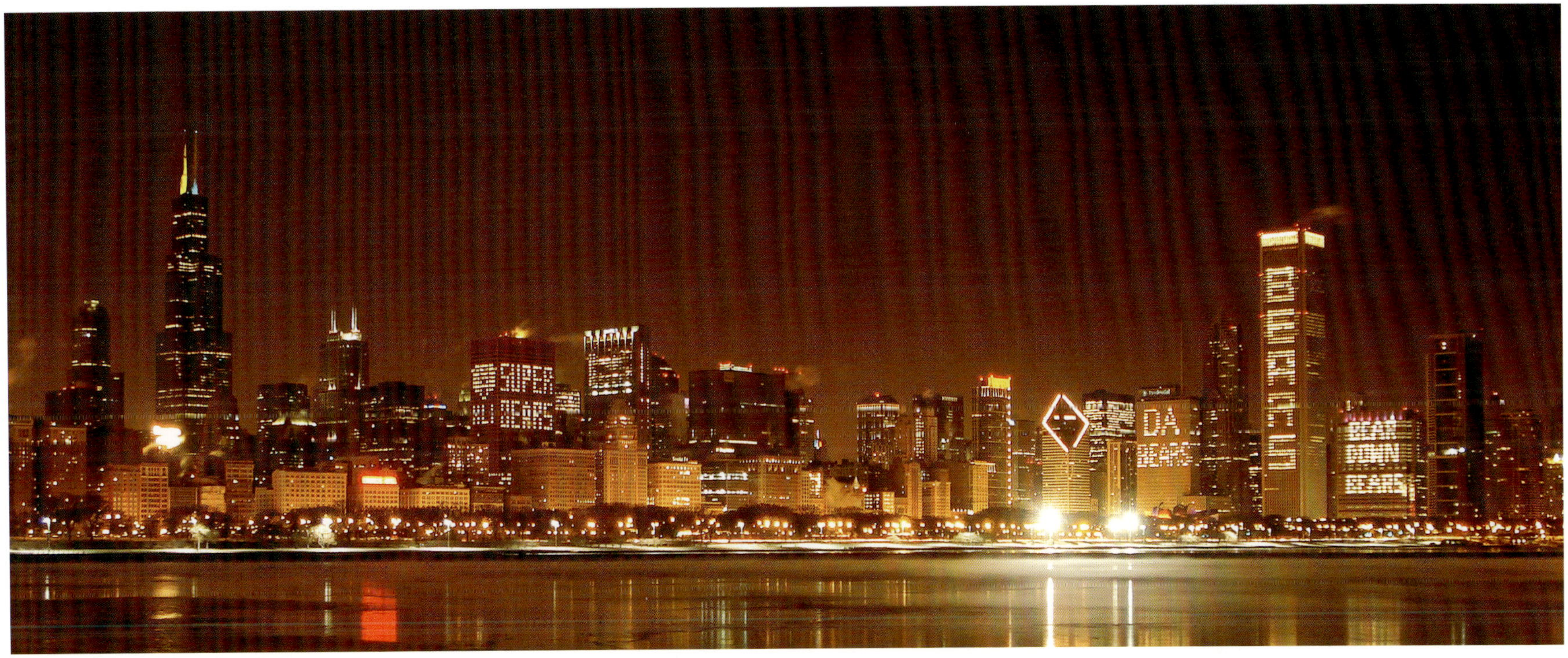
SUPER BEARS
DA BEARS
BEARS
BEAR DOWN BEARS

OPENING DAY *(previous top left)*
US Cellular Field
White Sox opening day, 2007.
📷 SEAN GALLAGHER

SOFTBALL AT GRANT PARK *(previous top middle)*
Warmer weather in Chicago means the start of softball season, and there's nowhere as picturesque of a setting as the big buildings while playing in Grant Park. 📷 ERWIN ARAOS

WRIGLEY AUTUMN SILHOUETTE *(previous bottom left)*
Classic fall view, without the Fall Classic.
📷 KEVIN DOOLAN

GO BULLS *(previous top right)*
Panoramic view of the United Center during halftime of a Bulls vs. Pistons game.
📷 MAURICIO MEJIA

SUPER BOWL SKYLINE *(previous bottom right)*
Northerly Island
Feeling warmth in sub-zero temperatures from a Chicago Super Bowl Sunday, February 4, 2007 at 12:00 am. 📷 RYAN SULLIVAN

THE KID *(right)*
United Center
Patrick Kane, 19, playing for the Chicago Blackhawks, March 2008. 📷 GEOFF HALLIDAY

THE WINDY CITY FLYER *(opposite)*
Bourbonnais, Illinois
Devin Hester, #23, affectionately known as "The Windy City Flyer," during the Chicago Bears' training camp in Bourbonnais, Illinois.
📷 SCOTT EVANS

Arts, Culture & Food

EXCLAMATION IN YELLOW *(top)*
Exclamation in yellow on the stairs to the front entryway of the Museum of Contemporary Art.
JENNIFER DICKSON

SKETCH *(bottom)*
Artist sketching among the masters at the Art Institute. DANIEL MESSICK

ORNATE FOUNTAIN *(following left)*
While visiting the Garfield Park Conservatory, I was surprised to see this ornate fountain just sitting there in a walkway, and couldn't help but make a photograph of it. JOHN CARUSO

★ **WINDOW BY TIFFANY** *(following right)*
A view of the Chicago Cultural Center's Tiffany glass window not long after it was restored.
BARTH RILEY

"I spotted this lady in red inside the Art Institute of Chicago. The color of her sweater next to the artwork on display called out for attention. I still wonder what she was doing.
— AARON BROWN/THE WOMAN SITS ALONE

THE WOMAN SITS ALONE *(opposite left top)*
Art Institute of Chicago 📷 **AARON BROWN**

JAZZ SILHOUETTE *(opposite left bottom)*
Westmont, Illinois
Salt Creek Ballet Company dancers. 📷 **SCOTT LEWIS**

MITCH CAVANAH *(opposite right)*
Pierrot Gourmet Restaurant
Sous Chef Mitch Cavanah serves a shrimp and mango salad at Pierrot Gourmet. 📷 **ANDREW HICKEY**

PHYLLIS' MUSICAL INN *(left)*
Wood and Division, Wicker Park
It's amazing how beautiful a dive bar can be when empty and bathed in winter's warm mid-afternoon sunlight. 📷 **SARAH RHEE**

TURKISH FASHION *(bottom left)*
A fashion show at Turkish Fest in Daley Plaza. 📷 **ROBERT TAMBURELLO**

★ **ZAP POW BAM** *(bottom right)*
Rosemont
An artist at Chicago Comic Con. 📷 **SHANYA SMITH**

LITTLE BOY RED? (left)
Near North Ave
Ocean Smith, a local boy turned McDoanld's global casting star. 📷 SHANYA SMITH

TREATY OF PARIS: DAN (opposite left)
Dan of Treaty of Paris at Metro.
📷 TORI LYNN MARTIN

DEREK TRUCKS (opposite right top)
The Derek Trucks Band performs at The Park West, Chicago, 2009. 📷 MARK MAHAR

LONNIE BROOKS BAND (opposite right bottom)
House of Blues (lower level) Chicago
Alligator recording artist Lonnie Brooks with his band, at a private party at the House of Blues Bar (lower level). He is still performing all over the world at age 75 and has been playing in Chicago for over 40 years. He has entertained thousands and we are lucky to have his sons Ronnie Baker Brooks and Wayne Baker Brooks carry the torch 📷 JENNIFER WHEELER

SUE (following left)
Visitors at The Field Museum consider the Sue exhibit. 📷 MATHEW SPOLIN

PROTECTED BY FIRE (following right)
Chicago Loop
Fire performers during Looptopia.
📷 YAN PRITZKER

Scapes of All Sorts

THIN RED LINE *(above)*
Western and Belmont
Just passing by... 📷 **BRIAN HAGY**

HOPPING AROUND (top)
Lincoln Square
My daughter hops on one foot in front of the historic former Krause Music Store, designed by Louis Sullivan. It's located next door to one of our favorite coffee shops, The Grind, and was the perfect spot for letting out some excess energy. **SARAH RHEE**

NEXT STOP (bottom)
North State Street
I spent enough time waiting for this shot that I missed the very bus I was shooting. Oh well... it was Chicago and a nice day for walking.
BRIAN CRISSIE

CHICAGO'S SKYLINE ABOVE THE CLOUDS (opposite left top)
This photo was taken from a vantage point overlooking North Avenue Beach, looking southeast towards the city skyline early one morning. **MARY ELLEN BRENNAN**

FIRST SNOW (opposite left bottom)
Adams and Wacker
The first snow marks the start of winter in downtown Chicago. **YAN PRITZKER**

VARIETY IS THE SPICE OF LIFE (opposite right)
Each building has its own personality. It's as if they are saying... look at me... no, look at me!
CRAIG SKORBURG

SATURDAY NIGHT ON THE MAG MILE (following left)
CTA buses may appear slow, but they can provide for a nice light show, streaking down Michigan Ave. **ERWIN ARAOS**

CLOUDS REFLECTED (following right top)
It was one of those amazingly perfect days: the light was right, the clouds were right, the subject was right. I made this exposure of an old CTA (Chicago Transit Authority) train car at a train and trolley museum in South Elgin, Illinois. **JOHN CARUSO**

RUSH-HOUR PEDESTRIANS (following right bottom)
Sometimes when I'm leaving the office at the end of the day, I like to photograph the rush hour pedestrians walking below the Willis Tower on Adams Street, between Wacker and Franklin. **JEFF PHILLIPS**

DARK CITY *(above)*
Adams and Canal
View from the 15th floor of the 200 S. Wacker building. 📷 **YAN PRITZKER**

FROM WACKER DRIVE *(opposite)*
Looking north from 111 S. Wacker Drive. 📷 **RUBIN ROCHE**

EMBOSSED CHICAGO *(top)*
State and Michigan
An abstract embossed Chicago. 📷 **DAVE RAUBE**

SCHOOL'S OUT *(above)*
31st and Kedzie
The forgotten Washburne Trade School. 📷 **CHUCK JANDA**

RAPID DEMON *(above)*
Oak Park
I just couldn't pass up this scene of parking meters and scrawled graffiti. 📷 **JOHN CARUSO**

CATALOG *(opposite)*
Oak Park
Card catalog used for reference materials at the Oak Park Public Library main branch.
📷 **SAM DICKEY**

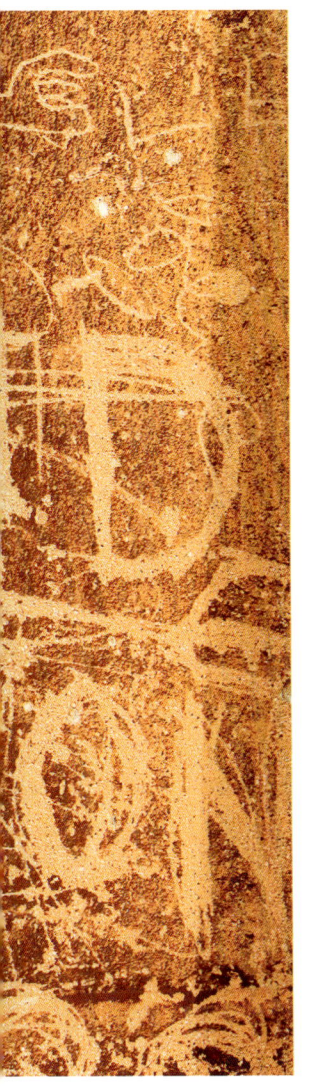

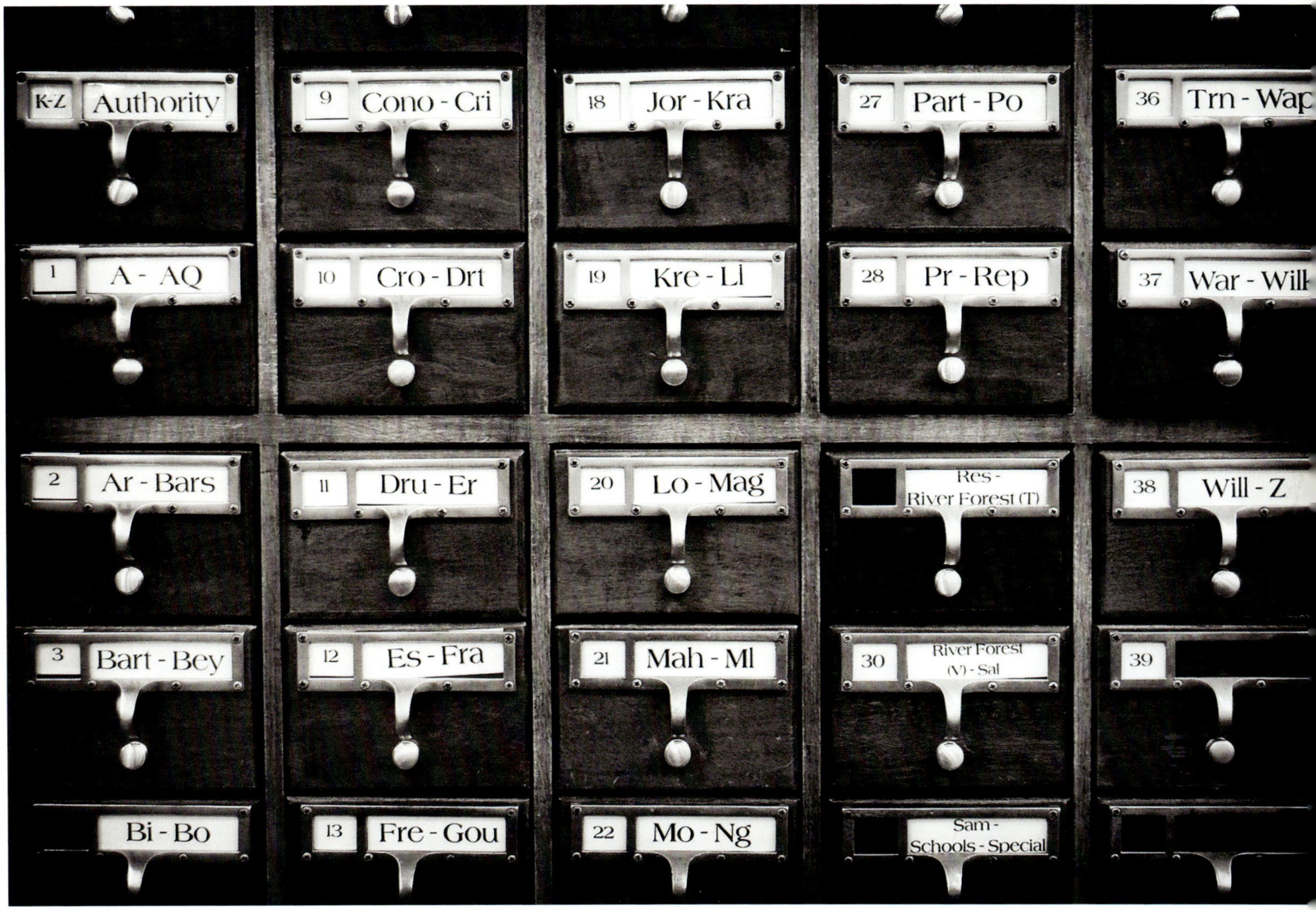

K-Z Authority
9 Cono - Cri
18 Jor - Kra
27 Part - Po
36
1 A - AQ
10 Cro - Drt
19 Kre - Li
28 Pr - Rep
37
2 Ar - Bars
11 Dru - Er
20 Lo - Mag
Res - River Forest (T)
38 Will - Z
3 Bart - Bey
12 Es - Fra
21 Mah - Ml
30 River Forest (V) - Sal
39
Bi - Bo
13 Fre - Gou
22 Mo - Ng
Sam - Schools - Special

MORNING FREIGHT (top)
Lisle, Illinois
A freight train passing through Lisle early in the morning. 📷 **MIKE UMBREIT**

WINTER YARD (bottom)
Roosevelt St. Bridge 📷 **SUSAN PHILLIPS**

TWO CTA TRAINS AWAIT DEPARTURE (opposite)
Kimball Station
End of the line! 📷 **LAURENCE PEARLMAN**

SNOWY PASS (following left top)
Hodgkins, Illinois
BNSF eastbound alongside Union Pacific westbound at Hodgkins on a cold winter's day.
📷 **JOE BALYNAS**

CSX AND THE CITY (following left bottom)
A CSX freight train heads past the California Ave. Metra yard with the downtown skyline in the background. Note Trump Tower under construction, summer 2008. 📷 **SAM DICKEY**

CHICAGO (following right)
View from the Western station on the Blue Line. 📷 **BRIAN HAGY**

> ❝ It was about 5 below zero and really miserable out when I saw these trains. I fished my camera out of my purse and braved taking a glove off to take this shot. It was so cold, the lens kept frosting!
> — **SUSAN PHILLIPS/WINTER YARD**

PANORAMIC SKYLINE *(above)*
Chicago skyline panoramic photo taken from the 11th Street Bridge on my walk to school one beautiful fall morning. This is a 3-shot panoramic photo taken hand held and stitched together. JEREMY CLIFF

CHICAGO CITY LIMITS *(left)*
Skyline from Sheffield & Diversey
As a storm photographer, I incorporate the sky in my city images as much as possible.
DAVID MAYHEW

FIRE IN THE SUMMER SKY *(below)*
Taken an hour after sunset, just as the last color was leaving the sky. Shot from Adler Planetarium. This consists of 11 shots (8 second exposures) in one row, stitched together.
JOHN CROUCH

PASSING CLOUDS *(opposite top)*
A different feel for a familiar scene, North Avenue Beach Pier, looking south.
ANDREW SECRIST

RIVER BEND *(opposite middle left)*
River Bend on the Chicago River
Chicago River at night. A composite of 11 images stitched together provides a very high resolution image capable of being printed in photographic quality at 17 feet wide, revealing intricate details. The image covers a 270 degree view. DAVID MAYHEW

SPECTRUM CHICAGO *(opposite middle right)*
Chicago Lakefront
Beautiful colors begin to rise up from the horizon as the sun goes to sleep. This photo captures the skyline of our beautiful city all lit up. NIM SHARON

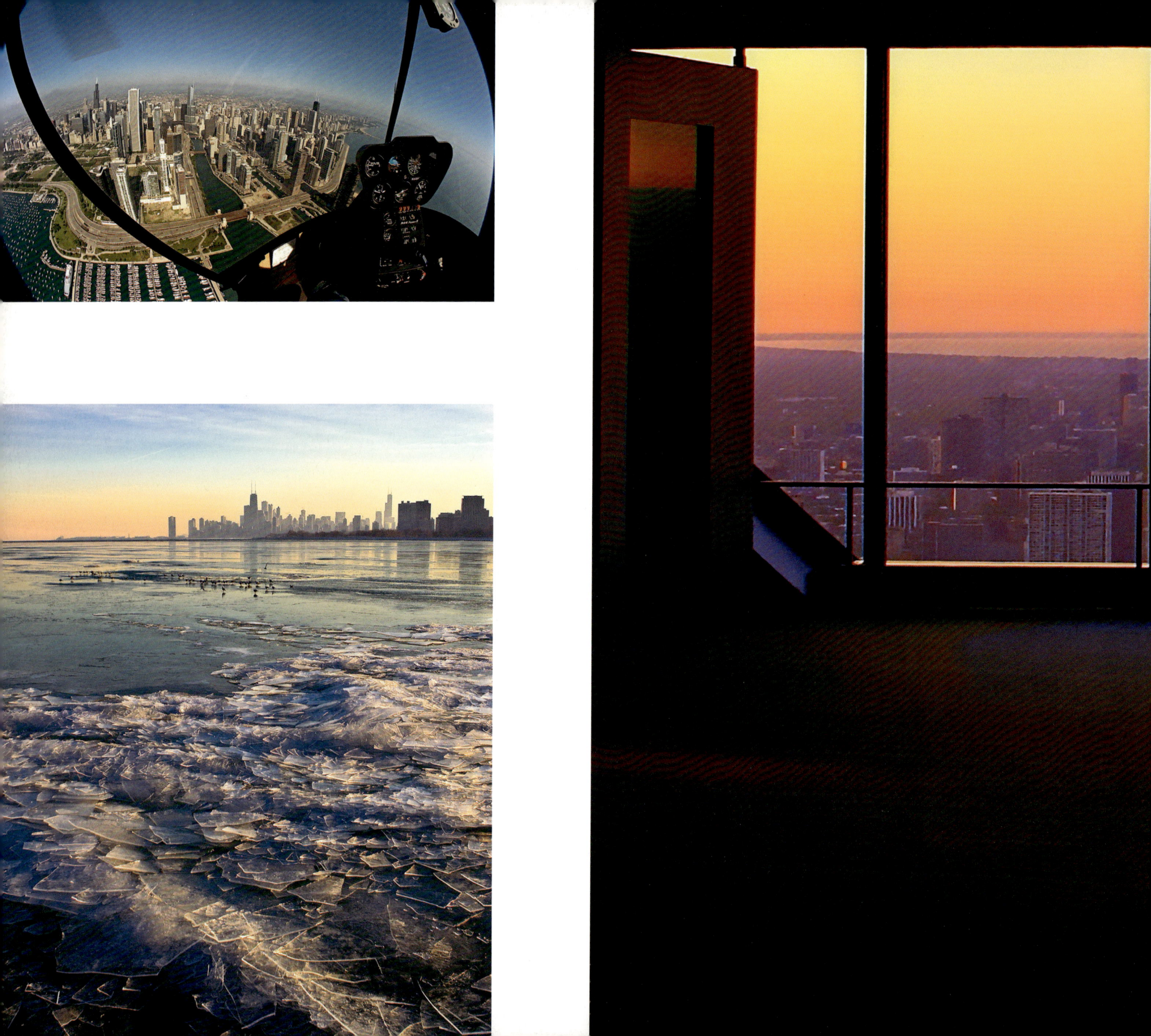

ONE AND WINDY CITY (above)
Lake Shore Drive, Monroe Park, early spring. 📷 **TATIANA KOUTCHMA**

FLYING OVER THE CITY (previous left top)
Taken with an 8mm wide angle fish eye. I love how the fish eye portrays Chicago on the curve of the Earth! It shows the tremendous growth from the core of downtown. 📷 **JASON LEWIS**

FROZEN CHICAGO (previous left bottom)
Ice sheets stack on top of each other as they are blown across Lake Michigan by southeasterly winds into Montrose Harbor.
📷 **DAVID MAYHEW**

OBSERVING NORTH (previous right)
The windows of the Hancock Observatory are marked to show the direction of the view. This couple was taking in the sights north of the Hancock just before sunset. 📷 **MIKE UMBREIT**

CHICAGO SKYSET *(above)*
Beach along Lakeshore Drive
Sunset over Chicago as the snow melts on
March 5th, 2009. 📷 **BRENDAN LEAHY**

**LOOKING NORTH
AT THE DRIVE** *(left)*
View looking north up Lake Shore Drive
from the John Hancock Observatory.
📷 **YVETTE FEVURLY**

STORM COMING (top)
South Loop
Clouds rolling in over downtown...
📷 DAN VERSON

★ **PANORAMIC** (bottom)
A Millennium Park panoramic. 📷 RUBIN ROCHE

**CHICAGO SKYLINE
AT NIGHT** (opposite)
A panoramic view of downtown at night.
📷 JORGE GERA

**SUNRISE OVER
LAKE MICHIGAN** (following left)
Shedd Aquarium
A wonderful reward for rising early... not an easy thing for a night person to do.
📷 ROSANNE MIEZIO

SUMMER BEACH (following top)
Taken at the beach over the summer.
📷 JEREMY CLIFF

CHICAGO SKYLINE (following bottom left)
A Chicago skyline shot across the water.
📷 JORGE GERA

31ST STREET (following bottom right)
A photo of 31st Street Beach just before sunrise, looking north toward the city.
📷 SVEN BROGREN

LOYOLA BEACH (above)
Cold lake air over warm sand. 📷 **MARK MULLIS**

BELMONT IN GRAY (right)
Belmont Harbor
Winter on the Lake. 📷 **JONATHAN WOOD**

ALONE IN THE LAKE (opposite top)
Montrose Beach
My friends decided to have fun in Lake Michigan. The day was misty and cold, but nothing stopped us from capturing beautiful Lake Michigan. 📷 **MICHELLE GANTNER**

STEAMY LAKE (opposite bottom)
North Avenue Beach
5 below zero is cold! My foot broke through the ice on the beach, so my foot was wet while trying desperately to shoot this shot quickly.
📷 **ANDREW SECRIST**

THE LAKE (previous left top)
A calm evening on Lake Michigan. 📷 **DAN VERSON**

LOYOLA BEACH (previous left bottom)
Loyola Beach. 📷 **MARK MULLIS**

WE HAVE ROTATION (previous right)
A storm front rolls in off Montrose Harbor. 📷 **PETE DOHERTY**

LIMESTONE WATERFALL (left top)
A waterfall feeds the historic Illinois and Michigan Canal east of Lemont, Illinois. 📷 **TOM GILL**

ESCAPE TO NATURE (left bottom)
Sometimes it's good to commune with nature. Take in the beauty that is the Morton Arboretum, Lisle, Illinois. 📷 **MIKE BAKER**

FOGGED IN (right)
Warrenville, Illinois
With all the recent fog the Chicago area has had, I have taken advantage of it by getting out there to capture it. This was taken at Blackwell Forest Preserve. Visibility was quite low. The island is barely visible beyond the end of the pier. 📷 **THERESA CRAMER**

★ LONG TIME GONE (above)
Evanston
One of my favorite local places to sit down and watch a sunrise over Lake Michigan is Lighthouse Beach. The combination of the rocks, the remnants of the old pier and the sound of the waves as they hit. These elements never cease to inspire me. **MANUEL DIAZ**

SUNRISE AT FABYAN (following left)
Geneva
Nice fall morning at Fabyan.
JONATHAN ROBSON

SUNRISE BRIDGE OVER SPRINGBROOK CREEK (following right)
Naperville, IL
Originally slated to be the home of a manufactured recreational lake, plans changed, and Springbrook Prairie is now 1,867 acres of swaying grasslands and restored prairies and wetlands and a great place to catch a beautiful prairie sunrise. **SCOTT EVANS**

LAKE MARMO *(above)*
Lisle, Illinois
The sun rising over the Lake Marmo Dam on a peaceful fall morning. **MIKE UMBREIT**

★ **INTO THE FOG** *(above)*
Naperville, Illinois
Naperville Riverwalk Bridge on a very foggy evening. 📷 **MIKE UMBREIT**

HARVEST SUNSET (top)
The sun sets in the autumn sky just off I-90, near Kane and McHenry Counties, during the evening rush to get home. ANDY ROUSEY

OPEN FIELD (bottom)
A field of dreams in Will County, Illinois.
CASSANDRA POZULP

WILMINGTON TORNADO (opposite top left)
A tornado tears through Wilmington, Illinois. The storm produced 6 or 7 different tornadoes on the way up to Gary, Indiana, June 7th, 2008. DAVID MAYHEW

TY WARNER PARK (opposite top right)
Westmont, Illinois
Three people enjoying the sunset at Ty Warner Park. ELIZABETH KUBIS

BRIDGE OVER LAKE MARMO DAM (opposite bottom left)
Lisle, Illinois
On a foggy morning at the Morton Arboretum, a look down the road that crosses over the Lake Marmo Dam. MIKE UMBREIT

MISTY MORNING GLOW (opposite bottom right)
It was a misty morning as the fog slowly lifted. But, when the sunrise hit at just the right angle, everything lit up to create a very surreal moment along the bike trail. GARY JACKSON

COUNTRY WINTERS (right)
I shot this in the far west suburbs of Chicago last winter. I love country drives all year round. I was searching for a barn mixed in with a lot of white snow and found it. 📷 **THERESA CRAMER**

WINTER SENTINEL (bottom left)
Grosse Point Lighthouse overlooks snow-covered dunes at Lighthouse Beach in Evanston.
📷 **MARK BALDWIN**

INFRARED CHICAGO (bottom right)
Fullerton at the lake. 📷 **MICHAEL MESKIS**

RURAL DUPAGE (top left)
Farm near Pratts Wayne Woods, DuPage County. MANUEL DIAZ

MERRY CHRISTMAS (top right)
Lake Forest's train station across from historic Market Square during the 2008 Christmas season. JOHN CROUCH

SEASON OF B&W PICTURES (left)
Monroe Park
December, when fun activities outside are often counted in minutes.
TATIANA KOUTCHMA

> "It still looks like old Europe to me.
> — CRAIG SKORBURG/WRIGLEYVILLE

WRIGLEYVILLE *(top)*
A Wrigleyville sunset. 📷 **CRAIG SKORBURG**

FOG OVER EAGLEBROOK *(bottom)*
Geneva, Illinois
Fog in Fox River Valley can be very heavy. This is a scene depicting a portion of the golf course that is a part of the Eaglebrook subdivision in Geneva. 📷 **DRAGAN PETROVIC**

FABYAN DUTCH WINDMILL *(opposite)*
The Fabyan Windmill is an authentic, working Dutch windmill dating from the 1850s located in Geneva, Illinois. The 68 foot, five-story wooden smock mill sits upon the onetime estate of Colonel George Fabyan, but is now part of the Kane County Forest Preserve District. In 1979, the windmill was listed on the National Register of Historic Places.
📷 **FERDINAND MARTIJA**

AUTUMN MORNING *(following left)*
A path through the autumn woods at the Morton Arboretum in Lisle, Illinois.
📷 **MARK BALDWIN**

A TOUCH OF GOLDEN SUN *(following right)*
Naperville
Taking a hike in some of the local preserves can seem like a trip to an exotic location.
📷 **MANUEL DIAZ**

" Seagulls racing toward a woman who feeds them at a certain hour of the day. How they know that the woman was approaching is quite a mystery to me. — **KEN ILIO/THE RACE**

FRESH CROSSING (previous left)
Cantigny Park, Winfield
It's tempting to be the first to cross this bridge the morning after a storm, eh? **BRIAN CRISSIE**

OUR NARNIA (previous right)
Taken on a very cold day at the Morton Arboretum in Lisle. It was actually getting pretty dark so I brightened it up with a long exposure. This so reminds me of Narnia. **CHRISTOPHER WILSON**

THE RACE (top)
Thorndale Beach **KEN ILIO**

UNTITLED (bottom)
Peggy Notebaert Nature Museum **NICKI BRANDT**

LADY BUG ALIGHTS ON LAMB'S EAR (opposite)
Elgin, Illinois
Lady bug, lady bug, don't fly away! **RENEE CYBUL**

SPRING FLOWERS *(opposite)*
Spring flowers at Palos Park, Illinois.
CASSANDRA POZULP

BLOOMING BLUE *(above)*
Glencoe, Illinois
Captured from the Chicago Botanical Garden
ALLAN DELOS REYES

Newsworthy

AND SO IT GOES (left)
Grant Park
Memorial Day 2007. "Eyes Wide Open." The exhibit focused on impact of the Iraq War by displaying a pair of boots for every soldier killed. 📷 BECKY MORRISSEY

BLUE LINE BREAKDOWN (bottom left)
CTA Blue Line
Walking on the edge, two blocks from the Clark and Lake stop, riders evacuate the Blue Line train after it breaks down and sparks fly.
📷 PETER THOMAS

★ **VIOLATION OF CODE**
#09-64-100(C) (bottom right)
Wicker Park
"Parking as to block access to/or efficient use of alley, driveway, or fire lane." The Red Ball Project visited Chicago in the summer of 2008. Chicago's finest were actually admiring the art rather than issuing a ticket. Nothing was staged, I was just in the right place at the right time. 📷 JONATHAN WOOD

STRUGGLING STUDENTS (above)
Students in Chicago are having a harder and harder time each year paying for college, Catholic school and school uniforms. This is just a product of the devastation in children in the Chicago areas. 📷 **DELISHA MCKINNEY**

THIS IS MY VOICE BUT YOU IGNORE MY CRY (opposite)
Taylor and Throop
A curious kid who used to go to the school in the background. 📷 **CAREY PRIMEAU**

★ **FACE OF AMERICA** (above)
Tears of joy and hope as Obama is announced the 44th President of the United States on November 4, 2008. 📷 **BRENDAN LEAHY**

A NATURAL LOOK (right)
One of the few members of the crowd that chooses to see the rally in Grant Park with his own eyes. Photo taken November 4, 2008. 📷 **BRENDAN LEAHY**

JESSE JACKSON AND PAT QUINN (above)
Kennedy King College
I stole some time away from helping my Dad cook at Real Men Cook 2009 to take some photos of Pat Quinn and Jesse Jackson supporting the Real Men Cook cause. 📷 **CHRISTOPHER WILSON**

KA-POW (left)
Brach's Candy Factory building is blown up as part of the creation of the movie "The Dark Knight" in 2007. 📷 **KYLE TELECHAN**

THE LIEUTENANT (far left)
CFD, Station #1 at 419 S. Wells
Lieutenant's helmet. 📷 **ROB PUTNAM**

Pets

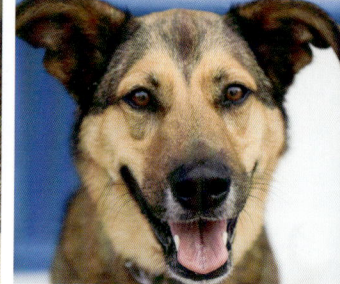
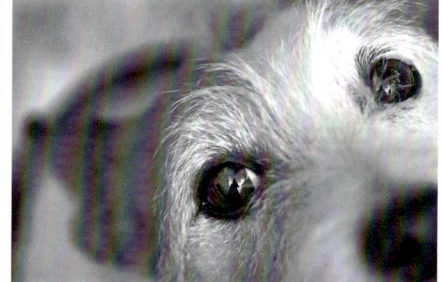

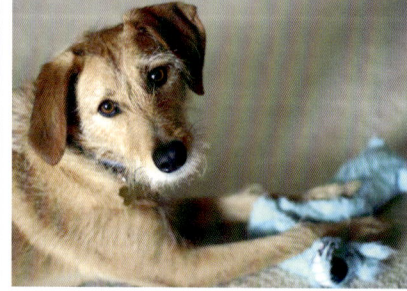

★ **BLACK BEAUTY** *(top left)*
Winfield
Beautiful creature. 📷 **JONATHAN ROBSON**

THE FARM *(top right)*
Horses are like people. They need to check out the new neighbors to find out just how friendly they are. Here, a Standardbred and an Arabian bond successfully and become great pals.
📷 **ROSANNE MIEZIO**

CAT IN A BOX *(left)*
Pilot! Photo taken August 10, 2009.
📷 **TRACY TUCHOLSKI**

ARE WE THERE YET, DAD? *(previous top left)*
Spencer riding in the truck with me.
📷 **GREG BAILEY**

HARD DAY'S WORK *(previous top right)*
After eating lunch, "Chappy" is enjoying the life of man's best friend with an afternoon nap.
📷 **SEAN TAYLOR**

SNOW DOG *(previous bottom left)*
Lisle, Illinois
A neighborhood dog who just loves being out in the snow. 📷 **MIKE UMBREIT**

TWISTER *(previous bottom middle)*
Naperville
Molly enjoying the mud! 📷 **JONATHAN ROBSON**

BACK SEAT DRIVER *(previous bottom right)*
Lincoln Avenue
Don't trust your mirrors! 📷 **STEVE YOUNG**

KIWI FRUIT *(above)*
Naperville, Illinois
Blue Fronted Amazon named Kiwi! 📷 **RICK CHIMNIAK**

★ **MIKO** *(left)*
Mayfair
Such a beautiful bird! 📷 **MARICEL CRUZ**

DAY TOGETHER *(following left)*
Lake Michigan
These two friends had a lot of fun together! 📷 **TATIANA KOUTCHMA**

ME & MY ALIEN *(following right)*
Glen Ellyn, Illinois
Daisy and Janessa. Daisy has the nickname "lil' alien" because of the Boston Terrier's quirky look. 📷 **JANESSA BULLEN**

Landmarks & Architecture

THE CHICAGO THEATRE (right)
Who wouldn't want to see Frankie Valli and the Four Seasons?
📷 **J. CHRIS CALLAHAN**

AMERICAN GOTHIC AT NIGHT (opposite top)
Pioneer Plaza, 401 N. Michigan Ave.
J. Seward Johnson Jr.'s sculpture, entitled God Bless America, depicts the farmer couple from Grant Wood's famous painting, American Gothic. On this beautiful winter night, the statue appears to be calmly overseeing the action of the passersby along Michigan Avenue, just North of the river. 📷 **LINDA HORTON**

IN THE BIG CITY (opposite bottom left)
Pa, I don't think we're in Kansas anymore. 📷 **LISA SULLIVAN**

SAVE THE SPINDLE (opposite bottom right)
This is a photo from the Critical Mass event on July 27, 2007, in an effort to help save the famous Dustin Shuler sculpture, "Spindle," that was located in Berwyn's Cermak Plaza. Record numbers of Critical Massers rode from Daley Plaza to Berwyn to show their support for the unique sculpture. 📷 **SEAN GALLAGHER**

BUCKINGHAM FOUNTAIN AT DUSK *(opposite top)*
The newly renovated Buckingham Fountain, at dusk, showing off its many new colors.
📷 **JASON LEWIS**

FACES OF CHICAGO *(opposite bottom left)*
Chicago's Millennium Park, a popular attraction that has so many things for us to see and do! 📷 **MARICEL CRUZ**

DANDELION *(opposite bottom right)*
The Dandelion fountain is one of the many recognizable landmarks in Naperville's Riverwalk. 📷 **MANUEL DIAZ**

SECOND CHILDHOOD *(above)*
Enjoying a respite from the heat at the Crown Fountain in Millennium Park. 📷 **KEN ILIO**

UNTITLED (above)
5 Soldiers at Adams and Wacker. 📷 **RUBIN ROCHE**

TRACTRICIOUS (left)
Tractricious is a sculpture that sits on the grounds of Fermilab in Batavia, Illinois. It was designed by Wilson and constructed by members of the Technical Support Section. The structure is comprised of 16 stainless steel outer tubes, made from scrap cryostat tubes from Tevatron magnets, and 16 inner pipes from old well casings. Each tube is free standing and designed to withstand winds up to 80 mph. 📷 **ERICA MARSHALL**

LOOK UP CHICAGO! (opposite)
Michigan and Chicago Avenues
A worm's eye view of Chicago's Water Tower and surrounding buildings. 📷 **KEN ILIO**

LOOP POST OFFICE *(left)*
Mies van der Rohe's Post Office stands in sleek contrast to its Loop neighbors. This building is located in Federal Plaza. 📷 **JOHN CROUCH**

ORANGE STAIRS *(right)*
Batavia, Illinois
Everything about Fermilab is artistic and interesting – it goes way beyond the neat architecture of the iconic Wilson Hall. There are many other interesting structures on the grounds as well. If you visit, take time to notice the details: the numbering of the floors in the stairwells in Wilson Hall, the power poles shaped like pi symbols and yes, even the stairs. It's an incredibly inspiring place to visit! 📷 **ERICA MARSHALL**

TOP OF THE WILLIS *(opposite left)*
No matter where you are in Chicago, you always look for the top of the Willis Tower. It becomes a habit after a while. 📷 **MICHELLE GANTNER**

SCRAPING THE SKY *(opposite right)*
Chicago's Sears Tower, now renamed the Willis Tower, signifies one of the most famous Chicago landmarks. The Willis Tower remains the tallest building in the United States. This photo captures the true 'skyscraper' essence of the tower as the antennae split the sunlight and passing clouds. 📷 **ALEXANDRE ROSEN**

BLUE REFLECTIONS *(following left top)*
Lake Point Tower is a photographer's dream. The outside edge of the tower is elevated which makes it easy to look directly up the side of the building. This photo was taken during my first visit and I still remember how amazed I was when I looked up. The reflection in the glass is the tower itself. 📷 **MIKE UMBREIT**

STONE FACADE *(following left bottom)*
You would be amazed at the patterns you can find in the architecture around Chicago. This is a photo of a building on Michigan Avenue.
📷 **CRITTER RETTIRC**

WINDOWS UNLIMITED *(following right)*
Look at all of those windows! Lake Point Tower has 11,310 double-paned windows. 📷 **MIKE UMBREIT**

AQUA (previous left)
The side of the Aqua condos simulates our connection to the beautiful waters that surround us. **CRAIG SKORBURG**

CITY REFLECTED (previous right)
Chicago's Wrigley Building reflected in the widows across the street. **JOHN CARUSO**

ABOVE THE CLOUDS (left)
Wacker Drive
Chicago's skyscrapers towering over the weather.
AMADOR VALENZUELA

BIG JOHN (right)
The John Hancock Tower. **DAVID HOOK**

LEANING TOWER YMCA *(left)*
Niles, Illinois
Twilight serenity. 📷 **JOHN MASTALERZ**

DOWN *(right)*
430 East Waterside Dr.
Stairs around the Aqua Building. 📷 **ROLANDO CERVANTES**

★ **DOWN TOWN** *(following left)*
As I walked down Chicago Avenue, I stopped in my tracks when I saw this wall heading down into the subway. I had my camera in hand and made a photo that, to me, will always remind me of the city.
📷 **JOHN CARUSO**

EARLY MORNING BEAN *(following right top)*
An early morning Bean photo. The clouds are blurry because the shutter speed was set to a few seconds. 📷 **SVEN BROGREN**

FROSTED BEAN *(following right bottom)*
Cloud Gate. 📷 **ERIK LYKINS**

S *(left)*
A shot of the famous stairs in the Chicago Museum of Contemporary Art. 📷 **CHUNSUM CHOI**

★ **CONVERGE** *(previous left)*
An 'L' train carefully navigates the tracks downtown in the Loop. 📷 **JOHN CROUCH**

SOUTHBOUND *(previous middle)*
Sears Tower and Merchandise Mart from the Chicago Avenue El stop, taken when it was still the 'Sears' tower. 📷 **CHRIS GANS**

TWISTING AND TURNING ALONG THE BROWN LINE *(previous right)*
This is a 20-second shot of two elevated trains passing each other along the Brown Line in Chicago. The red streaks are from the train going away from the camera and the blueish and greenish colors are from the train approaching my position. 📷 **JOHN CROUCH**

UNION STATION *(opposite top)*
Union Station. 📷 **TORI LYNN MARTIN**

CITY GRID *(opposite bottom left)*
The elevated tracks in the Loop form such orderly and elegant lines. 📷 **JOHN CROUCH**

TO ALL TRAINS *(opposite bottom middle)*
A late night at Union Station. 📷 **RYAN DAVIS**

COLUMNS *(opposite bottom right)*
Union Station. 📷 **JONATHAN WOOD**

> I love seeing the landmarks from a different point of view. — **HAROLD BLUM/SIX ON THE BRIDGE**

SIX ON THE BRIDGE (above)
Millennium Park
I was visiting friends on East Randolph Street and they generously offered me time on their balcony to take some pictures and enjoy the park. 📷 **HAROLD BLUM**

GOLDEN PIER (left)
Navy Pier as seen from Lake Michigan
The sun filters through the clouds on a June evening, casting a golden glow over Navy Pier.
📷 **RYAN DAVIS**

ROOKERY STAIRCASE (previous left)
LaSalle & Adams
The Rookery staircase was designed by Frank Lloyd Wright as part of the lobby's 1905 renovation. 📷 **JOHN CROUCH**

★ **ST. STEPHEN'S** (previous right)
Interior of St. Stephen's Church in Hyde Park. 📷 **DANIEL BARTEL**

BURNHAM PAVILION (left)
Burnham Pavilion by Ben van Berkel of UNStudio in Chicago's Millennium Park. 📷 **DANIEL BARTEL**

BRIDGEHOUSE (bottom left)
Chicago IL
Chicago Bridge House and River Museum. 📷 **DELISHA MCKINNEY**

CALDERRA (bottom right)
Loop
Looking up... 📷 **EUGENE FELIX**

BURNHAM PAVILION (opposite)
Zaha Hadid's Burnham Pavilion in Chicago's Millennium Park.
📷 **DANIEL BARTEL**

MEDAL OF HONOR (following left)
Near Navy Pier
I caught the perfect reflection at the gates of Milton L Olive III Park on a cloudy and misty morning. 📷 **GAUTAM DESAI**

1893 (following right)
The Entrance to the Chicago Stock Exchange by Louis Sullivan.
📷 **JEREMY CORDELL**

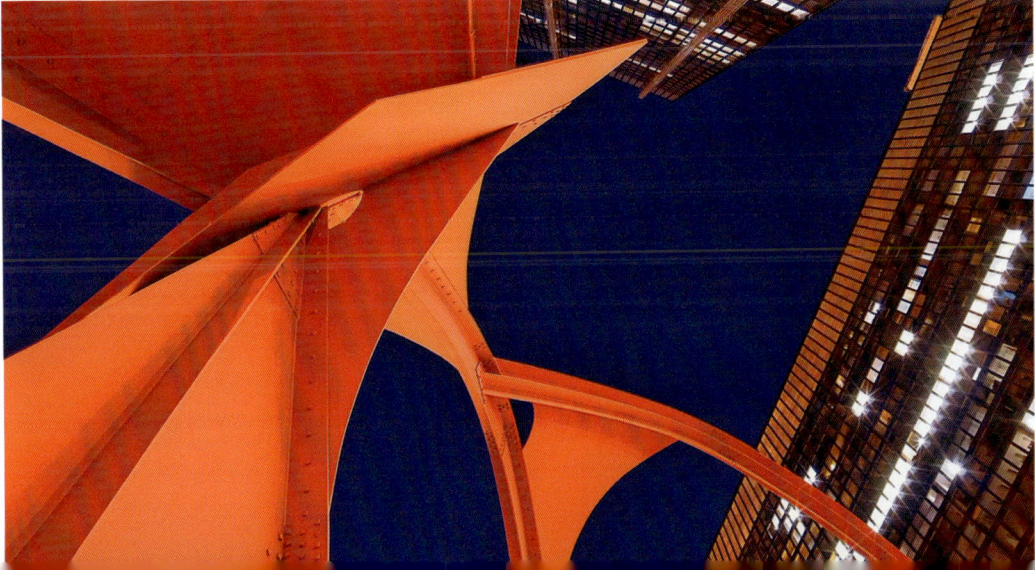

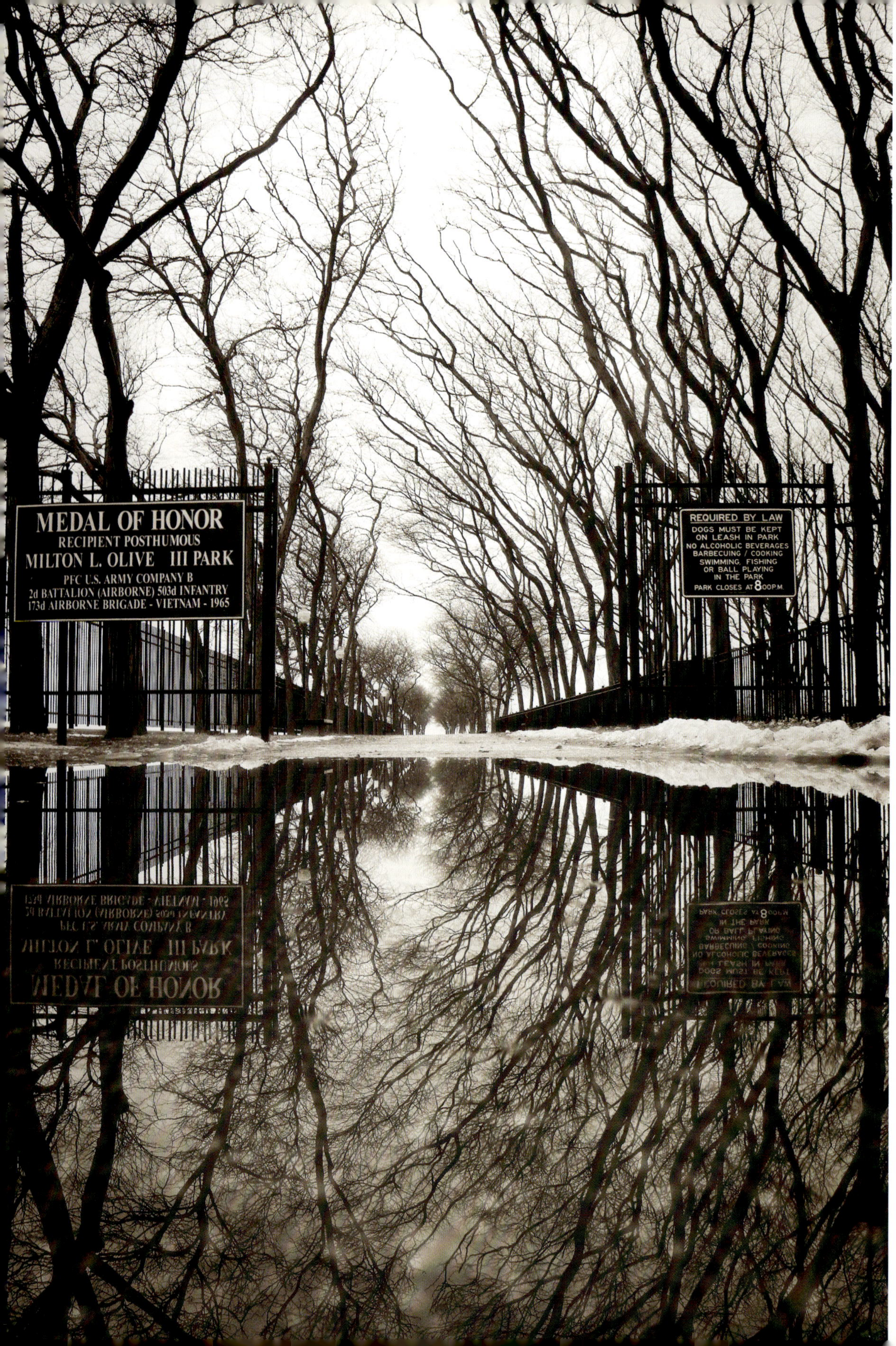
MEDAL OF HONOR
RECIPIENT POSTHUMOUS
MILTON L. OLIVE III PARK
PFC U.S. ARMY COMPANY B
2d BATTALION (AIRBORNE) 503d INFANTRY
173d AIRBORNE BRIGADE - VIETNAM - 1965
REQUIRED BY LAW
DOGS MUST BE KEPT
ON LEASH IN PARK
NO ALCOHOLIC BEVERAGES
BARBECUING / COOKING
SWIMMING, FISHING
OR BALL PLAYING
IN THE PARK
PARK CLOSES AT 8OOP.M.

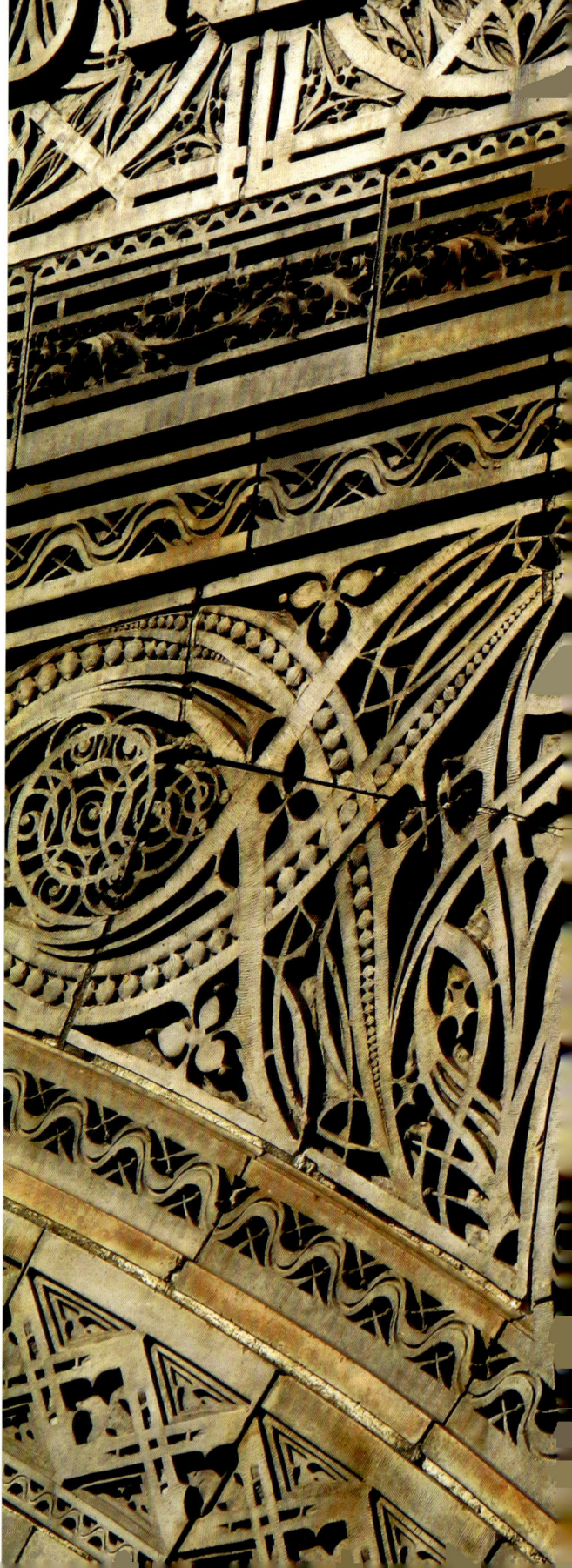

PERFORMANCE EXTRAORDINAIRE (above)
There is nothing quite like a beautiful summer afternoon, a comfortable spot in the grass, and beautiful music filling the park at the Jay Pritzker Pavilion. Chicago, there's no city like it!
SAMUEL BARR

PRITZKER AND CITY (left)
Millennium Park's Jay Pritzker Pavillion after a performance by the Joffrey Ballet.
SARAH PETERS

JAY PRITZKER PAVILION (far left)
The Jay Pritzker Pavilion provides an amazing place to enjoy concerts with state-of-the-art sound and the magnificent Michigan Avenue as a backdrop. NATHAN MAYBERRY

Recreation & Celebration

FLIGHT TEAM (left)
On media day for the 2009 Air and Water Show, I got to go up with the Lima Lima Flight Team. They flew over downtown Chicago and Lakefront. What a ride! I'll never forget it!
ERICK CLARK

SPIN CITY (bottom left)
In a city that works, there is always a spin.
ANTONIO (TONY) CASTILLO

CONTROL FREAKS (bottom right)
Lakefront
The Chicago Air and Water Show.
JAMIE REED

UNTITLED (above)
I took this picture during the Air and Water Show. I was most struck by how the red props and white contrails contrasted so vividly with the blue sky. 📷 **JEFF STEVENSON**

LET ME OUT OF HERE! *(above)*
Chicago River on Michigan
Rubber duckies at the Duckie Race on the Chicago River for the benefit of Special Olympics of Illinois, August 8, 2008. KEN ILIO

VOLLEYBALL (above)
A volleyball net at sunrise, North Avenue Beach. 📷 **NIKKI JOHNSON**

WHITE POSTS (right top)
Dawn at North Avenue Beach volleyball courts. A few hours later, the nets will go up and hundreds of Chicagoans will play some friendly, and perhaps a few not so friendly, matches!
📷 **BENJAMIN OLIVER**

FISHING THE GOLDEN SEA (right bottom)
Lakefront at Montrose
Fishing at dawn. 📷 **JONATHAN WOOD**

REACHING FOR THE CLOUDS (opposite)
Early in the morning at the top of a Lincoln Park hill. 📷 **DEBBIE CABRERA**

FLY BABY FLY (above)
Navy Pier
A study in contrast: The young woman in the foreground, hands free, smiling, barefoot, legs swinging freely, flowing hair and behind her what appears to be the complete opposite. Older woman, hands firmly holding the chains, legs crossed, shorter hair, wearing shoes. These women are riding the Wave Swinger at Navy Pier Chicago.
CHRISTOPHER WILSON

ROUND AND ROUND AT NAVY PIER (left)
Navy Pier
One of the attractions at Navy Pier that takes you back to your childhood. It's still fun just watching it go round and round while hearing children scream with delight in the background. ROLOUR GARCIA

NAVY PIER (opposite)
Navy Pier at night. MARIUSZ PIEROG

CHICAGO (above)
Fireworks and the Chicago skyline.
JEFF LEWIS

★ **FIREWORKS BY THE LAKE** (left)
Navy Pier fireworks. JORGE GERA

VICTORY (following left)
Chicago Criterium, 2009. TOM FENNELL

**IT ALL COMES
DOWN TO THIS** (following right)
Remington Lakes Sports Complex
A moment frozen in time at the Balln Basketball Tournament, summer 2008, Bolingbrook, Illinois. CHRISTOPHER WILSON

HARBOR FOG (above)
Chicago Harbor
Fog rolling into the Harbor, taken from the Sears Tower. 📷 **JEREMY CORDELL**

ST PATTY KAYAKER (previous left top)
Kayaker in the Chicago River after the St. Patrick's Day river dying celebration.
📷 **SEAN GALLAGHER**

BOATS IN A HARBOR (previous left bottom)
One thing I've always loved about Chicago is the way the lakefront has been utilized. These boats in Burnham Harbor are just one example. 📷 **JOHN CARUSO**

RIVER GREEN (previous right)
The waters of the Chicago River receive a vibrant dose of green each year for the city's St. Patrick's Day celebration. 📷 **AURORA SAMAR**

STUNNING WELCOME *(above)*
Sailing into the Chicago skyline at sunset.
GREG JOHANSON

FALL FISHING (above)
A crisp autumn morning on Batavia. A pair of fishermen try their luck on the foggy Fox River.
📷 **MANUEL DIAZ**

TWO-HOUR TOUR (opposite top)
A sudden change of weather during a waterborne Chicago architecture tour was unfortunate for passengers, but it was an opportunity for photographers. 📷 **JEFF PHILLIPS**

BURNHAM HARBOR SUNRISE (opposite bottom)
Burnham Harbor, taken very early in the morning while the waters are still and the reflections nearly perfect. 📷 **JAMES WATKINS**

YOUR TROPICAL PARADISE (above)
Oak St. Beach on a beautiful summer day.
📷 **KEN ILIO**

HUSKY HEROES (opposite)
Lisle, Illinois
Husky Heroes is an annual event at The Morton Arboretum. 📷 **MIKE UMBREIT**

★ **NYE** (following left)
Auditorium Theatre
Umphrey's McGee on New Year's Eve 2008. At midnight they did a giant balloon and confetti drop. 📷 **TORI LYNN MARTIN**

HEADING FOR HOME *(following right top)*
Rounding the final bend, heading for home at Arlington Park. 📷 **PETER WELDON**

THE AFTERMATH *(following right bottom)*
Paper cups, Chicago Marathon, 2005.
📷 **KEN ILIO**

" Teams of Siberian Huskies display their amazing abilities to large groups of spectators all in an effort to promote adoption of homeless Huskies. — **MIKE UMBREIT/HUSKY HEROES**

THE SCREAM (opposite top left)
A beaver at Lincoln Park Zoo. This was taken the opening month of the kids area. **DAVID MAYHEW**

SMILE (opposite top middle)
Brookfield Zoo
Smile! You're on candid camera. **JOHN MASTALERZ**

BEST FRIENDS (opposite top right)
Brookfield Zoo
These mandrills certainly seem to enjoy the company as they groom each other. **ROSANNE MIEZIO**

ONYX (opposite bottom left)
Brookfield Zoo's primate house is a beautifully natural looking place that houses some real beauties. Onyx, here, is certainly one of them! **ERICA MARSHALL**

TWO ZEBRAS (opposite bottom right)
An abstract look at two juxtaposed zebras at Lincoln Park Zoo. **DAVID APRIL**

BROOKFIELD ZOO (left)
An elephant at Brookfield Zoo.
FRANCISCO MONTES

SHEDD AQUARIUM (right)
I invite you to visit the Shedd Aquarium.
TERRY ANGELONI

Prize Winners

When picking from 28,144 photos, it's difficult to nail down what separates the best from the rest, especially when so many photos are so good. To help, we enlisted thousands of local folks to vote for their favorite shots. The response was epic: 2,388,443 votes were cast. The voting helped shape what would eventually be published in this book. Along the way, the votes produced the prize winners below. Here's a brief explanation of how prizes were determined:

People's Choice: This one's as simple as it sounds. The photo that gets the highest score, according to how folks voted, is given this award. We picked a different winner for the Editors' Choice award, but we think local folks are pretty smart too, so we wanted to reward the photo that people like the most. This is also one of the ways we figure out the grand prize.

Editors' Choice: This award goes to the photo our editors determine to be the best in a chapter. Sometimes it'll be a photo that fits the chapter so well that it stands out above the rest. Other times it could be a photo that is technically excellent. Our editors poured over submitted photos daily during the contest and were constantly thinking about which photo should be the "Editors' Choice." Our editors also helped pick the grand prize photo from a pool of People's Choice photos.

People's Choice in Friendly Faces
PHOTO BY MIKE COLEMAN
page 11

People's Choice in Sports Spirit
PHOTO BY JEAN LACHAT
page 17

People's Choice in Arts, Culture & Food
PHOTO BY SHANYA SMITH
page 29

People's Choice in Scapes of All Sorts
PHOTO BY MANUEL DIAZ
page 63

People's Choice in Newsworthy
PHOTO BY JONATHAN WOOD
page 83

People's Choice in Pets
PHOTO BY JONATHAN ROBSON
page 90

People's Choice in Landmarks & Architecture
PHOTO BY JOHN CARUSO
page 112

People's Choice in Recreation & Celebration
PHOTO BY JORGE GERA
page 136

Editors' Choice in Friendly Faces
PHOTO BY CLIFTON HENRI
page 10

Editors' Choice in Sports Spirit
PHOTO BY ERWIN ARAOS
page 18

Editors' Choice in Arts, Culture & Food
PHOTO BY BARTH RILEY
page 27

Editors' Choice in Scapes of All Sorts
PHOTO BY MIKE UMBREIT
page 67

Editors' Choice in Newsworthy
PHOTO BY BRENDAN LEAHY
page 86

Editors' Choice in Pets
PHOTO BY MARICEL CRUZ
page 91

Editors' Choice in Landmarks & Architecture
PHOTO BY DANIEL BARTEL
page 119

Editors' Choice in Recreation & Celebration
PHOTO BY TORI LYNN MARTIN
page 148

Grand Prize Winner
PHOTO BY JOHN CROUCH
page 114

Cover Shot Winner
PHOTO BY RUBIN ROCHE
cover, page 54

Photographer Directory

Capture My Chicago was made possible by local photographers who were willing to share their talents with the rest of us. Here's a list of everyone you'll find in these pages and on the DVD. If you know any of these folks, give them a ring and say thanks for the great book!

(Photographers with Web sites in following list.)

MIKE ABRAM
TONY ABREGO
GABRIELA ACEVEDO
DANA ACOSTA
MIKE ADAMS
PAT ADAMS
JOY ADAMS
JAMES ADAMS
TIM ADAMS
PAM ADAMSKI
PRATIK AGRAWAL
LINDA AGUILAR
DREW AHRENS
ELIA L. ALAMILLO
SHELLIE ALBERT
FAITH ALBERTSON
NOHEMI ALCALA
ASHLEY ALDEN
EAN ALEXANDER
XHENGIS ALIU
DEBRA ALLEBACH
DENISE ALLEN
JENNIFER ALMANZA
JULES ALTENBERG
LUIS ALVARAY
RITA ALVAREZ
STEFANI ALVAREZ
MARYA AMANULLAH
ROB AMBROZIAK
MICHELE AMBROZIAK
YUL KEITH AMERSON
DEBRA AMSDEN
ART CHRISTIAN AMURAO
SARA ANAYA
CELIA ANAYA-CORONADO
RYAN ANDERSON
MA ANDERSON
REBECCA ANDERSON
SAMANTHA ANDERSON
RENEE ANDERSON
NANCY ANDING
SEBASTIAN ANDINO
GREG ANDREAS
TERRY ANGELONI
ART ANGELOPOULOS

MARCOS ANTONIO
WENDY ARMINGTON
BOB ARMSTRONG
SHANNON ARMSTRONG
ROMY ARRIETA
DIRIM ARSLAN
TINA ARTEAGA
JAMES ARTEAGA
EDUARDO ARTIGA
RIK ARTIM
BRIDGET ARTMAN
MEGAN ASHLEY
MARGOT ASHWORTH
SAMUEL ASSEFA
JOHN ASTIN
JIMMY AYALA
DANNI B.
JOYCE BABBITT
WILLIAM BACH
JUDY BACHLEDA
KRISTIN BACZKIEWICZ
ANITA BAGLEY
DAPHNE BAILLE
ASHLEY BAKER
RAQUEL BALDERAS
PHILLIP BALICK
STEVE BALLINGER
JOHN BALZER
ANINDYA BANERJEE
GALAB BANKOV
KIM BANKS
MOSHE BANTASAN
HENRY BARCIKOWSKI
BARBARA BARG MEDLEY
MICHELLE BARNES
DAVE BARNETT
VICTOR S BAROCAS
MARK BARON
GABINO BARRERAS
DOREEN BARRETT
NANCY BARRETT
JANET BARRIENTOS
ALBERT BARTKUS
MARY KAY BARTON
CAROL BARWACZ

DEBBIE BATES
TORI BATES
NICK BATTAGLIA
KARINA BAUER
KRISTIN BAUER
JASON BAX
HELEN BAXTER
LISA BEALL
KAREN BEAN
ANTHONY BEARD, SR.
DAVID BECCO
MELENIE BECKER
LAUREN BELL
EDWARD BELL
AMY BELL
JOY BELL
TERRY BELL
SHEILA BELLEN
DEBBIE BELLER
RICK BENDER
SARAH BENDIXON
HOLLIE BENEDIK
DAVID BENJAMIN
ALEX BENNETT
DAVID BENSON
BOB BENSON
RITA BENTZLER
JILL BENZAQUEN
CINDY BERARD
MARY CAROL BERCHMAN
MICHAEL BERDEAUX
SOFIA BERG
SHERWIN C. BERGER
REBECCA BERKLEY
JESSICA BERKLEY
KATE BERMAN
MIHAELA BERNARD
CAROL BERNIER
CHAD BETTENCOURT
PAM BEVER
KAREN BEZOLD
KASIA BIELA
JANET BARRIENTOS
KELLI BIGEL
GERI BIGGS
HAL BILODEAU

ANNE BILOS
TIM BIMMERLE
DEBBIE BIRINGER
BRUCE BISHOP
JAY BITTERMAN
SEAN BLAHA
TIM BLANKENSTEIN
DANIEL BLANNER
MARY BLAUSEY
BRANDI BLOWERS
DIANNE BLUNK
COURTNEY BOBINSKY
SHAWNEE BOCK
KATHIE BOCK
MATTHEW BOCKUS
CHARLES BODNAR
BARBARA BOES
LEANNE BOGOFF
SIDNEY BOGUE
MAEGEN BOHAC
DENISE BOKSA
EMILY BOLIN
BRENDA BOLTON
CHRISTINA BONANNO
C RUSSELL BOND
MERREL BOOKER
OLIVIA BOOKSHESTER
OLGA BORJA
THOMAS BOTTOM
KAYLEE BOURLAND
JEANNIE BOUTELLE
JODI BOVA
BETH BOVEN
DAN BOWLING
JENNIFER BOWMAN
CLIFF BOYCE III
BOBBI BOYD
PEGGY BOYTOR
SHIRLEY BRACH
KATHY BRADLEY
CHRIS BRADLEY
JASON BRAINERD
NICKI BRANDT
BARB BRANN
KATHLEEN BRANT

DARLA BRAYTON
CHRISTIE BRENDAL
MARY ELLEN BRENNAN
KAREN BRESLIN
BUDDY BRESSLER
CAROLYN BREWER
GREG BRIDWELL
DARIUS BRIGHT
SARA BRINK
KRISTYN BROOKS
DEREK BROUWER
REBECCA BROWN
JODI BROWN
DON BROWN
COURTNEY BROWN
RACHEL BROWN
ANNIE BROWN
V K BROWN
FRANKIE BROWN
TONY BROWN
GLORIA BROWN
CHRIS BROWN
MANDEE BROWN
CINDY BROWN
ERNEST BROWN
ELAINE BROWN
TIMOTHY BROWNE
GUS BROWNE
JOYCE BRUEN
CARL BRUNS
WILLA BRYER-DOUGLAS
KURT BRZUSZKIEWICZ
CARA BUCCIARELLI
ROBERT BUFFO
VANESSA BUHOLZER
AMANDA BUHRANDT
KAY BUNAGAN
CHRIS BUNSEN
KIM BUNTING
ELIZABETH BURBATT
AARON BURKE
MOLLIE BURKIEWICZ
TONY BURROUGHS
BARRY BUTLER
LAURA C.
HYACINTH CABAEL
DEBBIE CABRERA
ARLENE CADA
COURTNEY CAFLISCH
ROD CAIN
NATHAN CALABRESE
DAVID CALARIE
BRADIE CALHOUN
JAMES CALLAHAN

ELENA CALOCA-NORMAN
JOHNNA CALVILLO
LISA CAMPBELL
PATRICIA CAMPBELL
CHRISTINA CAMPBELL
IAN CAMPBELL
PHYLLIS CAMPBELL
SUZANNE CAMPION
DAVE CAPP
DAVE CAPPERINO
FRANK CARDENAS
LISA CARDINALE
MARIA CARDOW
SCOTT CAREY
JACK CARLSON
BRAD CARLTON
GRADYTHE CARR
KELLEY CARR
BRENT CARSTENSEN
SANDRA CARTER
SHELLY CARTER
TONI CARUSO
LINDA CASALETTO
CHRISTINA CASEY
ROBERT CASEY
JORGE CASIANO
GRANT CASLETON
JENNICA CASTON
QUETZALLI CASTRO
KRISTINE CAVALLONE
DAN CAVAZOS
PHYLLIS CERNY
JENNY CHANDLER
EMILY CHANDLER
SUSAN CHAPLIK
VIVIANA CHAPMAN
KYLE CHARABOWSKI
DALE CHARLES
CHARLENE CHAUSIS
JAMIE CHEATHAM
PETER CHERR
CATHY CHESTER
WANDA CHILLEMI
RICK CHIMNIAK
ALI CHINLUND
MAX CHOPOVSKY
DIANA CHRISMAN
MARINA CHRISTIANSEN
AUSTIN CHRISTINA
KATIE CIEBIEN
JIM CIESLIK
SUSAN CIGELNIK
LANETTE CIMBALA
ERICK CLARK
TERRY CLARK

DEBORA CLARK FAIRFAX
ROGER CLAUDIO
JOHN CLEAVELAND
NIKOLE CLEVENGER
LAURA CLIFFORD
OLIVER CLOTHESOFF
SANDY CODY
DON COGLIANESE
JERRY COKER
JAMES COLE
DIANNE COLEMAN
STEPHANIE COLEMAN
CHRISTINA COLEMAN
STEPHEN COLLETTE
ALBERT COLLEY JR
KEVIN COLLIER
JUDY COLONERO
SID COLTON

MARISSA COLVETT
KARYN CONCANNON
JEFF CONDREN
DIANE CONMY
TAMARA CONRO
ANDRIA CONROY
WILLIAM CONTA
SUE CONWELL
MARILYN COOK
NICK COOPER
KEVIN CORCORAN
JEREMY CORDELL
KARL CORDES
ANITA CORDES
DOUG CORELLA
ED COREY
JIM CORNO, JR.
JUNIOR CORTEZ

FRANCINE COSENTINO
JOANNE COSTOPOULOS
JOSHUA COX
MICHELLE COX
VINNIE COZZI
NANCY CRAIG
LEE CRANDELL
BRIAN CRAWFORD
JANET CREMENS
FRANK CRESCENZI
JOE CRESSMAN
ED CRESTONI
BRUCE CRITELLI
MARILYN CROCKER
JAMES CRONIN
LOU-ANNE CRONIN
ALISSA CRONIN
LATOYA CROOKS

LORIE CROUSE
KYLE CRUICKSHANK
GILBERT CUA
SHARON CULLARS
DANIEL CULLIVER-DODD
NICOLE CUNNEA
MEL CUSIMANO
RENEE CYBUL
GLENNA CYTRYNBAUM
WALTER E. CZORNYJ
DAVID D
LOUIS D'ARIENZO
MARY DAHLBERG
STEVE DAHLKE
RAY DAHLQUIST
BRIAN DAHLSTROM
MIKE DAICHENDT
ANNE DAILEY

One of Capture My Chicago's most active groups:

Chicagoland Digital Photography Meetup
http://www.meetup.com/Chicago-Digital-Photo/

1,504 Photos
146,526 Votes

MARICAR ABELLA
JULIO AGRON
MAREK AKSAMIT
B. ANDRÁS
ERWIN ARAOS
JOE ASENCIOS
MIKE BAKER
ANDREW BARICKMAN
MELENIE BECKER
TERRY BELL
DEBBIE BELLER
MICHAEL BENNETT
SVEN BROGREN
DIANE BRONSTEIN
DAVE CAMERON
SANDRA CARTER
MATTHEW COGLIANESE
JAMES COLE

JAMES COLE
MIKE COLEMAN
ED CRESTONI
KATHI DEMASI
MELANIE DIAZ
PATRICIA EPPS
TOM FENNELL
CHRISTINE FITZPATRICK
CYNTHIA FUSCO
SHARON GAIETTO
MARIE GILBERT
JODI GOLDSTEIN
YASMIN GOSIENGFIAO
TAMMY GREEN
GABRIELA GUILLERMO-GARZA
RICK HICARO JR.

KATRIN HUMMEL
GREG JOHNSON
NIKKI JOHNSON
LYNDON JOHNSON
KATTALINA M KAZUNAS
HEATHER KEIGHER
KURT KRAMER
MIRIAM KRAVIS
TEMI KUJORE
GENE LILLIE
RICKEY LOGGINS
JULIA LUCAS
CINDY MAMMOSER
WENDY MCDANIEL
KAREN MCKINLEY
MATTHEW NORTH
GREG NOWAK
MICHAEL J. NYCHAY

CHRISTOPH G. OLESCH
SAMANTHA ORTIZ
ANNE P
TERESA PEEK
DRAGAN PETROVIC
CRITTER RETTIRC
BARTH RILEY
BETTY LARK ROSS
LORI SWERDLOW
ROBERT TAMBURELLO
ANNA TRIVINO
MIKE UMBREIT
BENJIE URBINA
GABRIEL V
TIFFANY WHISLER
BEN WONG
SERWA ZIADEH
EMELIA ZUCCHERI

LINDA HORTON

153

ABENA SHARON DALE	NICHOLAS DODARO	MYRON ELLIOTT	BARBARA FLAWS	MARK GARCIA	INDARS GRASBERGS	DIANA HARRISON	MARIANNE HOSPODAR	STEVE JERZYK	BETTE ANN KELLY
BOB DALTON	JOHN DODGE	BARBARA ELLIS	CHERYL FLETCHER	ROSE GARCIA	RITA GRAVEL	FRAN HART	LEON HOUSE	DEREK JESKEY	KRISTEN KELLY
JESSICA DALTON	GLADYS DOEBELI ROCOURT	KARYN ELLIS	NONA FLORES	DORA GARCIA	ISAAC GRAY	JOE HARTL	KATHERINE HOWARD	CARLOS JIMENEZ	MICHAEL KELLY
CLARA DAMPTZ	LESLIE DOLAT	JANET ENG	JESSICA FLORES	RICK GARD	JAN GRAZIANI	KATRINA HARUCKI	NANCY HOWE	KOSINSKI JOANN	CAL KENDALL
WALLY DANCZAK	LISA DOLATO	JOE ENGELS	ANNE FLYNN	AARON GARDINER	JOHN GREENWALD	JOHN HASSEL	KARMELA HOWELL	GREG JOHANSON	FRANK KERES
CHRIS DANNER	MARYANN DOLL	AARON ENGLER	SUZANNE FLYNN	JONI GARFIELD	NICK GREGOR	ROGER HASTINGS	ADAM HOWITT	STACY JOHNSON	NICK KERLEY
ELIZA DAVILA	ANDREW DOMINGUEZ	MARS ENNS	MADELYN FOGARTY	DAWN GARRETT	JOE GREMAL	BRITT HAUGEN	J HOYER	GREG JOHNSON	AARON KERNES
RASHAD DAVIS	MARK DONNELLY	LESLIE ERICKSON	DANA FOLEY	SUSAN GARTSHORE	WILL GRENDAHL	DAN HAUSCHILD	QIANFAN HUANG	KRISTINE JOHNSON	AMY KERR
PAUL DAVIS	SHEILA A. DONOVAN DONOVAN	ROBERT ESCOTO	CHRIS FOREST	DIANA GARZA	MIKE GRENKE	KEVIN HAUSFELD	RUDY HUDSON	DEE JOHNSON	TODD KERSH
ALICE DAVITT	KEVIN DOOLAN	MARIA ESPINOSA	JOE FORMELLA	TONY GAUL	MARKETA K. GRESL	HEATH HAYS	PETER HUETSON	TIM JOHNSON	DINAKAR KESAVAPILLAI
MARJORIE DE LA ROSA	LAURA DOOLEY-TAYLOR	EDUARDO ESTRADA	PETE FOSKARIS	MITCH GAWLIK	CHARLENE GRIDER	JENNIFER HEALY	JOYCE HUGHES	LEE JOHNSON	MIRA KEYES
BARBARA DE LACEY	CAROL DORSEY	KRISHA ETHERIDGE	MARIANNE FOSNOW	SANDY GELATT	KENNETH GRIFFIN	BRYANT HEART	MARIANNE HULBERT	VIRGINIA JOHNSON	MANSOOR KHADIR
BEN DE LEON	WES DORSZEWSKI	KAREN EVANS	JENNIFER FOSS	TRISH GEMINN	MICHAEL (SLIM) GRIM	KENAN HEBERT	KATRIN HUMMEL	LISA JOHNSON	FAHAD KHAN
CINDY DEAL	KATHERINE DOTY	JOHN EVANS	RONALD FOSTER	TINA GERA-DURSO	KAREN GRONKA	TERRENCE HEIDEN	LEIF HUNTER	JASON JOHNSON	MUBASHIR KHAN
DEBBIE DEAN	KRISTIN DOUCETTE	GERARD M. EVANS	SUE FOSTER	JOSEPHINE GERARDI	SHELLEY GROSLAND	MICHAEL HEIMLICH	B HUNTER	ARLENE JOHNSON	MARY KIAUPA
TRENT DEAN	BILL DOWGIALLO	KENNETH EYER	ERICA FOSTER	PATRICIA GERBER-BORNHOLT	REEM GROSS	TOM HEINRICH	NANCY HUNTSHA	COREY JOHNSRUD	ROBERT KIDD
VALERIE DEANER	KATE DOWNING	MEG F	NED FOWLER		JUDY GROSS	AMY HEINRICHS	SARI HURTIG	ALEX JOMARRON	CATHERINE KIERUZEL
JUSTIN DEARE	ERIN DOWNS	LEANDRA F.	SANDY FOX	LORNA GERMAN	KATIE GROSSART	MICHELLE HELGESEN	TERRY HUSER	JENNIFER JONES	DALE KIFFEL
JO ANN DEASY	S DOYLE	RACHEL FABRO	PATRICK FRANCIS	JENNIFER GERRY	CLIFFORD GROST	GERALD HELLER	JIMMY HUSKE	TONY JONES	MIKE KILLION
DIDI DECHEVA	JULIA DOYLE	JODI FACCHINI	IVO FRANCO	ALAN GERSTNER	TED GUARNERO	DOROTHY HENDERICK	MARY HUSKE	FRANCES JONES	SEUNG KIM
JENNIFER DECKER	MICHELLE DRABEK	JOE FALKENBERG	GENEVIV FRANK	KEN GETTY	CELINE GUERRERO	KEVIN HENNAGER	HISHAM HUSSAIN	HENRY JONES, JR.	MARISA KINN
BECKY DECKER	VIKKIE DRAWANT	CINDY FANDL	JENNIFER FRANK	PAULA GIANNINI	ANGELA GUERRIERI	THOMAS HENNEMAN	RICHARD HUSSEY	PAULA JORDAN	BAR KIRBY
JOANNA DEJESUS-MELARA	SUSAN DRECHNEY	ELLEN FARBER	JOHN FRANTOM	NANCY GIARDINA	DEBBIE GUIDA	GISELE HENNINGS	PAUL HUTCHISON	JAMES JORDAN	LYNN KIRCHHOFF
M ESTELA DEL TORO	JANE DRENNEN	MARTIN FARKAS	BILL FRANTZ	NICO GIBSON	DANA GUNDERSON	GEORGE HENRY	ROBERT HYMAN	CAMILLE JORDAN	KATHLEEN KIRKPATRICK
ANNE DELA CRUZ	RICHARD FAULKNER	RICHARD FAULKNER	CHANDRA FRASER	MICHAEL GIBSON	PATTI GUNKELMAN	MARTIN HENRY	JOSEPH B HYMES III	DEBBIE JORGENSEN	RICK KISLA
DONNA DELANEY	JOEL DRESSELHAUS	KARA FAWBERT	MARISSA FRATTINI	KC GIESSEN	ERIN GUNTHER	STEVE HERLIHY	ANTHONY IACUZZI	HANNAH JORJORIAN	KYLE KISSEL
KIERAN DELANEY	TAMMY DRING	CAROL FEDERIGHI	GREG FREEDMAN	CHRISTINA GIFFEY	ANU GUPTA	CARMEN SILVIA HER-NANDEZ	MARIYA ILLARIONOVA	PETER JOSEPH	GREG KLAIBER
ALLAN DELEON	ARIANNA DUBOVIK	BILL FEELY	KAITLYN FREESE	GIOVANNI GIGLIOTTI	SETH GUTING		ERIN INDOVINA	STEVE JOYCE	CAROL KLEIN
KAREN DELVECCHIO	PATRICIA DUCHARM	ILANA FEKETITSCH	ERIC FREIBRUN	ED GILBERT	DON GUZAN	PETER HERNANDEZ	JULIE INFELISE	LAUREN JUDGE	GEORGE KLEPPER
MIKE DEMAR	CATHIE DUFF	SARAH FELDMAN	LEN FRIDDLE	NICOLE GILHOOLEY	LINDA HAAKSMA	NATHAN HERREMANS	JOSH INGLIS	SANDY JUNGKUNTZ	KRIS KLIMEK
MICHELLE DEMARCO	BERNIE DUFFETT	DAVE FELLBERG	CHAYA FRIEDMAN	MARVIN GILLESPIE	ROBERT HAARMANS	JULIE HESTER	LYNN INNIS	SANDY JUNTA	TRACY KLOSS
KATHI DEMASI	REBECCA DUKE	BRAD FENISON	ALLAN FRITZ	JAY GILLILAND	MANDI HAGELINE	JEAN HICKEY	ALDO IRIZARRY	AARON JURA	RON KLOSS
KAVITA DEODHAR	RICHARD DUNCAN	WILLIAM FENNESSEY	KARMEN FRLAN	KRISSIE GILLIS	DOLORES HAGER	JO FREDELL HIGGINS	CATHERINE IRONS	JOANNE JURGENS	KIM KLYCZEK
KRISTY DEROSE	EBONIE DUNIVER	GAIL FERGUS	PHILLIP FUGATE	SARAH GINDVILLE	MICHAEL HAGER	CHRISTOPHER HILL	ARIEL ISENBERG	MOSHE KAGAN	BONNIE KLYCZEK
ANTHONY DERRICK	PAUL DUNNE	TRACEY FERGUSON	SHARON FULLINGTON	CHRIS GINGRICH	ANNETTE HAHN	CARRIE HILL	JEFF IVENS	ROGER KAHLE	JUDITH KNIE
GAUTAM DESAI	DARCY DURKEE	RUBEN FERNANDEZ	LONNIE FULTON	JAI GIRARD	EVELYN HAKL	LINDA HILL	ANIA J	MELISSA KAHN	METABOLISM KNIGHT
CYRIL DESMOND	DEBORAH DURNWALD	LISSETTE FERNANDEZ	STEPHANIE FUNK	LOU GLANTZ	JASON HALEY	JENNIE HILLS	GERALYN JACKMAN	REGINA KALBACH	BILL KOCH
ALAN DETTLAFF	RICHARD DUSLACK	DEIDRE FERRON	SHARON FYKE	CATHY GLEASON	JAYNEE HALL	KANPIWAT HIMACHAROEN	VELVA JACKSON	TED KALISZ	DENNIS KOCIENDA
VENKAT DEVIREDDY	MICHELLE DYKSTRA	YVETTE FEVURLY	JORIE G	JOHN GLOVIK	JOHN HALL	HOLLIS HINES	STEVEN JACOBS	BILL KALNES	JOE KOHLEY
JORDAN DEWEESE	JANINE DZIEROZYNSKI	CRAIG FIEDLER	JONATHAN GABEL	AMBER GOCKEN	DAVID HALPERIN	JEAN HO	TINA JACOBSON	ALLISON KAMEN	ANNE KONCHAN
TRAVIS DEWITZ	AARON EAKIN	RICHARD FIMOFF	VIRGINIA GABEL	CARNEZ GODFREY	ASHLEY HALPIN	LEAH HODGES	ERIK JACOBSON	JONATHAN KAMIN	MICHELE KOOYENGA
SILVIO DI PAOLO	ABBY EARL	ROBERT FINCH	AVAH GABRIEL	RANDY GOLLAY	ESTELA HAMMOND	BRENT HOFFMAN	JERRY JADE	SCOTT KANE	TIM KOPP
ANDY DICHTER	JUDY ECHTERLING	JACK FINEBERG	AARON GAFNER	MARORA GOLTSMAN	CEDRIC HAMPTON	DIANA HOGAN	SIMON JAGODA	EVAN KANE	BETTY KORABIK
JOHN DICK	BARB ECKARD	WILL FINEBERG	CHERYL GAINES	INES GOMEZ	DUANE HANACEK	LEE HOGAN	JENNIFER JANIK	SWETA KAPADIA	LINDSEY KORTH
JOSH DICKEMANN	MELANIE EDBURG	JIM FINNIGAN	MARIO GALINDO	SUSAN GONDEK	JEANINE HANDLEY	JONATHAN HOGUE	STAN JANKOWSKI	KENNETH KAPELLA	JOHN KOSACZ
LARRY DIECKMANN	DONNA EDER	RALPH FIORE	REGINA GALLAGHER	FELIX GONZALES	EMILY HANNAN	PATTY HOLECEK	DALE JANUS	MOLLY KAPERICK	NANCY KOSCHIK
NICHOLE DIEHL	SHERRI EDWARDS	AUDREY FISCHER	BRIGID GALLAGHER	KEN GONZALES	PAMELA HANNIGAN	JERRY HOLK	ROSS JANUSZYK	AL KAPLAN	JUDY KOSCIOLEK
BILL AND CINDEE DIETZ	STEFANIE EDWARDS	LIESEL FISCHER	RANDALL GALLEGOS	HUGO GONZALEZ	DAYNA HANSBERGER	STAN HOLLENBECK	SUE JARRELL	JOHN KARELS	ADRIENNE KOSTREVA
JOANNE DIGUIDO	KRISTEN EGAN	WALTER FISHER	HALEY GALLINA	BOB GOODMAN	TOM HANSEN	MICHELLE HOLLINS	ARLENE JARZAB	DAVID KASNICK	TATIANA KOUTCHMA
REBECCA DILLAVOU	CHICAGO EH	MARY PAT FISK	JENNIFER GALLOY	MELISSA GOODNOUGH	JENNIFER HANSON	ANDREW HOLLOWAY	BEN JASEK	LAUREN KASPAR	J KOZICKI
KELLEY DILLNER	PHIL EICHAS	ERIN FISKE	ALEXIA GALLUCCI	ALVIN GORDON	PAM HARNACK	CONNIE HOLT	SUE JEFFERSON	LEE KAUFMAN	DAN KRAEMER
EDWARD DILORENZO	ANDREW EISENBERG	STACEY FITCH	CHRIS GALVEZ	BETH GORDON	BECKY HARPER	DAVID HOOK	JEANINE JEFFERSON	CAROL KAY	JOE KRAJEWSKI
JINWEN DING	MARY EKERN	BETTY FITZGERALD	KELLEY GAMBERA	DAVID GORE	JULIE HARRIGAN	JESSICA HOOVER	JEJE JEJE	KATTALINA M KAZUNAS	LESLIE KRAKORA
SAMANTHA DITE	ANDY ELBERT	KATHY FITZGERALD	ANIL GANDHI	JASON GORSKE	JEN HARRIGAN	DEBRA HOOVER	KEITH JENKINS	DOUG KEALLY	LAURA KRANTZ
ANGELA DIVIRGILIO	PATRICIA ELIZONDO	PAUL FITZGERALD	VIPIN GANDRA	YASMIN GOSIENGFIAO	ADAM HARRINGTON	SANDY HOPE	SCOTT JENNER	AMANDA KEEGAN	MOLLY KRAUS
ARTHUR DIZON	PRATHER ELLEN	ANNIE FITZMAURICE	JOHN GANNON	STEPHAN GOURDOUZE	DEBRA HARRIS	KATHLEEN HOPPE	KEN JENNINGS	HEATHER KEIGHER	JAMIE KRAUS
SANDRA DJORDJEVIC	JOHN ELLINGSON	GAIL FLAGLER	VIVIAN GARAY	DEB GRAHAM	JIM HARRIS	AZIZA HOSEIN	ANTHONY JENNINGS	AMY KELLER	KARL KRAUSE
DANA DOBROVITS	A. ELLINGTON	ANNE-MARIE FLANNERY	ANA GARCIA	WES GRANGER	ANDY HARRIS	SHERRI HOSKINS	KRYSTLE JENSSEN	LIZ KELLER	RENEE KRECZMER

DEB KRESNICKA
BRIGITTE KRIEMAN
SRIRAM KRISHNAN
CLIFFORD KROENING
ANDREW KROWCZYK
CHERYL KRUEGER
ZVEZDANA KUBAT
ELIZABETH KUBIS
NICOLE KUCERA
CANDACE KUCZMARSKI
STEVE KUENSTLER
TEMI KUJORE
BOB KURASZEK
KAREN KUSEK
JOHN KUSH
KENNY KWAN
MICHELLE LACEY
BARB LACEY
WILLIAM C LADAS
MATTHEW LAFLAMME
LANIE LAGMAN
DEBORAH LAKE
BRIDGET LAKE
PATTI LAMANTIA
JAMES LAMBDIN
KAREN LAMBERT
RICHARD LAMBERT
JEN LAMBETH
BETH LAMBRECHT

SUE LAMCZYK
BRITTANI LAND
ASHLEY LANE
GREG LANG
DEBBIE LANG
CAROL LANG
JEFF LANGE
TONY LANGSTON
DENNIS LANNON
ELLEN LAPERLE
LUCIA CRISTINA LARA
BOB LARAMIE
YOLANDA LARRY
DEBRA LASKY
KEVIN LASTER
ERIC LAUDERDALE
KAFESJIAN LAURA
CATHY LAVARDA
IRA LAWRENCE
SCOTT LAWRENCE
APRIL LAWRENCE
SANDI LAWRENCE-BROGREN
ALANNA LAZAROWICH
DANIEL LEAL
CANDICE LEDMAN
RICHARD LEE
CHERYL LEGRAND
LYON LEIFER
CHERYL LEMMY

GABRIELA LEN
DAWN LENNON
VICTOR LENTINI
PHIL LENZO
AMY LESKO
LUZ LETAMENDI
KAREN LEVANG-EVINGER
ALISON LEVAR
COOKIE LEVINSON
MARVIN LEVINSON
AUDREY LEWIS
WILLYEM LIBERMAN
TONY LIDDI
JESSICA LIES
LORI LIGHTHALL
GENE LILLIE
BILL LINDEN
HELEN LINDSEY
DWIGHT LINDSEY
ED LISS
STEVE LIVESEY
MARY LOCHNER
SHANNON LOFTIS
EMILY LOGUE
MATT LOHMUS
EMILY LOHRBACH
MATT LOHRBACH
ANGELA LOIACONO
DONNENE LOID

HELEN LOOD
BARBARA LOPEZ
IRENE LOPEZ
GABRIELLE LOPEZ
LIZ LORANCA
CHRISTINA LORANZ
MICHAEL LORY
BRIAN LOUNSBURY
MIKE LOVATI
SCOTT LOYD
JILL LUCAS
AMY LUCAS
BRIAN LUCHT
YOLANDA LUCKEY
RENEE LUGO
BRIANNE LUKOWSKI
DONNA LUNA
KAIREE LUNA
LINDSEY LURIE
GAIELLE LUSK
CAROLINA M
MARIA MACHIN
CORNELIUS MACK
BRAGADEES MADAMBAK-KAM
PATTY MADSEN
DEAN MAGDALIN
LAURA MAGNAVITE
MARYANN MAGNO
ROBIN MAHER

ROBERT MAHER
ALLYSON MAISEL
EDWARD MAJERCIN
AMANDA MAKAREWICZ
ASHLEY MAKAROWSKI
GREGOR MAKSYMIW
GEORGE MALAMIS
ALEX MALASIG
ANU MALETIRA
LEROY MALONE
MICHAEL MALONEY
JERLYN MALOY
ERICA MANCUSO
ELLIOT MANDEL
MICHAEL MANLEY
KELLY MANTECK
PK MANZI
MARLA & GREG MARGELEWSKI
CAMILLE MARIANI
MARY MARKS
APRIL MARKS
RICHARD MARKWART
ROSE MARLOWE
ROSAURA MEDINA
MIKE MAROULIS
ASHLEY MARQUARDT
JODI MARQUITH
JA N MARSCHKE
JERRY MARSH
ARLETTE MARTIN
ROSANNE MARTIN
VICTORIA MARTIN
ART MARTIN
JOBE MARTIN
DANNY MARTIN
BETZAIDA MARTINEZ
EVELYN MARTINEZ
MARIANNE MARTINEZ
ROBERT MARTINEZ
PATRICK MARTINO
RICH MARVAN
MARY LOU MARZ
AMANDA MARZO
RON MASTERS
PATRICIA MASTERTON
ANUPAMA MATHUR
KATHY MATTERN
KELLY MATUSIAK
PAULA MATZEK
MARY ANN MAURER
MICHAEL MAVRIDIS
DEBBIE MILLER
RAYMOND MAXIMO
GEORGE MAY
BENNETT MAYER
DEBBIE MAYNARD
LINDSEY MAYNARD
MAUREEN MAYS
MARY MCARTHUR

TOM MCAULIFFE
LAUREN MCCADNEY
IAN MCCALL
ELIZABETH MCCARTHY
TRICIA MCCOY
WENDY MCDANIEL
TERI MCDERMOTT
KIM MCELHENY
MARC MCGOWAN
MATHEW MCGRATH
HORACE MCGRIER JR
CATHY MCGUIRE
KAREN MCKINLEY
DELISHA MCKINNEY
LESLIE MCLAIN
JAMES MCLARTY-LOPES
PATRICK MCLAUGHLIN
KERRY MCLENAHAN
BILL MCMAHON
DIANE MCNULTY
EMORY MEAD
DERRICK MEADOWS
KELLY MEADOWS
ROSAURA MEDINA
JOHNATHAN MEDLEY
EDWARD MEEHAN
ED MEEHAN
ALISSA MEKAMI
ROXANA MENDEZ
APOLINAR MENDOZA
GUS MENOUDAKIS
MARK MERAVY
ERICKA MERCER
JUDITH MERRITT
TINA METE
ANITA METTILLE
P. MEYNEN
DENNIS MICHAELS
BARB MICHAELS
STEVEN MICHALS
GLORIA MICHALSKI
GEORGE MICHELSEN
CHRIS MIDDLETON
GREG MIDURA
ROSANNE MIEZIO
CHRIS MIKA
TED MILENKOFF
JIMMY MILLARD
CARY MILLER
MELISSA MILLER
DEBBIE MILLER
DARCY MILLER
KIESHA MILLER
CHRISTIE MILLER
LORETTA MILLER
GARY MILLER
ERICA MILLER
WENDY MILLER

KATHERINE MILOSEVICH
JUDY MINTEL
PAUL MINX
JANET MIRANDA
KAMRAN MIRZA
JANET MISITI
FLAVIU MITAR
PATRICIA MITCHELL
STEFAN MITITELU
PARISA MOALLEMIAN
JOHN MOBLEY
APRIL MOK
KAREN MOLNAR
CORINNA MONTEMAYOR
TONI MOON
RENEE MOORE
MEL MOORE
ROSE MOORE
RICH MOORE
SONJA MOORE
THOMAS MOQUET
SUSAN MORAKALIS
CHAZ MORALES-WILLIAMS
JAMES MORAN
JOAN MORANGE
KELLY MORGAN
MELANI MORGAN
RICHARD MORGAN
DEBI MORITZ
RONALD MORRIS
JENNIFER MORRIS
ALEXIS MORRIS
ZACHARY MORRISON
BECKY MORRISSEY
DAVID MORRONE
KRISTIN MORROW
THOMAS MORTIMER
HECTOR MOSQUEDA
VIVIAN MOST
JYOTI MOTTIER
LUKE MOUSTAKAS
FRANK MROCZKA
BEN MUCIEK
MALGORZATA MUDJER
RAY MUELLER
SHANNON MUELLER
GEOFF MUELLER
JANIS MUHAMMAD
PIUS MULVEY
JENNIFER MUNOZ
ANDREW MUNSON
KAREN MUNTER
TERRI MURPHY
ARIEL MURPHY
ANN MURRAY
BERNARD MURRAY
MINDY MURRAY
PATTI MUSIALEK

DAVID MUSSATT
L. FOLEY MUTH
KENNY MUZZEY
AMANDA MYERS
CAROLYNN NAGEL
EDA NAR
BARTOLO NAVA
HEATHER NEAL
TIM NECAS
KAITLIN NEHLS
DALE NEHRING
MIKE NELSON
BILLY JOE JIM BOB NELSON
SANDRA NELSON
LINDA NEMETH
STACEY NETKO
ARNALDO NEVES DA SILVA
SANDI NEWMAN
MICHAEL NGARIMU
JUDITH NICHOLS
CATHY PALMER
TONI NIELSEN
ANASTASIA NIKOLAS
MAX NITCH
SONY NOE
JUNE NOLAN
JULIE NOLAND
JEAN NORMAN
STEVE NORRIS
MATTHEW NORTH
JANICE NORTH
JOE NORTON
KAREN NOVOTA
PAUL NOVOTNY
LINDA NOWAK
GREG NOWAK
JAMES NOWAK
KAREN NUZZO
JITEN PATEL
MELANIE PATRIC
RYAN PATRICK
KELLY O'BRIEN
LUCREZIA O'BRIEN
LINDA O'CONNELL
KATHLEEN O'DAY
JENNIFER O'DELL
TRACY PAUL
MARY O'GRADY
MARY E O'KIERSEY
PATRICK O'NEIL
MARK OBRIEN
SHANNON OCHOA
LAURA ODUM
RACHEL OEFELEIN
DEBRA OGORZALY
MARK OKONSKI
MICHELE OLDS
CHRISTOPH G. OLESCH
RANDY OLINSKI
DAVID OLIVA
BENJAMIN OLIVER
DEBBIE OLSEN

LAURA OLSEN
DEBRA OLSON
ROBIN OMALLEY
JENNIFER ORFUSS
DENISE ORLUCK
KELLIE ORR
JENNIFER OSWALD
DOUG OTTERNESS
EMILY OWCZARZAK
SCOTT OWSIANY
SRIKANT P
LIZA PABON
JOHN PACEWIC
R PACHTER
JORGE PAEZ
JOHN PAIGE
MARY PALACIOS
PATRICIA PALAZZO
PATRICK PALCZYNSKI
CATHY PALMER
AL PALMER, III
TONI NIELSEN
PAULA PALTER
MOTTINGER PAMELA
MEGAN PAMPENELLA
GERI PANICKO
DAVID PAO
THOMAS PAQUETTE
PAMELA PARA
ASHISH PAREKH
IRIS PARKER
TANYA PARKS
DAN PARKS
RONALD PASKO
LEONARDO PASTORE
PRATIK PATEL
YASIN PATEL
JITEN PATEL
MELANIE PATRIC
RYAN PATRICK
JEAN PATTERSON
PAULINE PATTERSON
JOHN PATTERSON
TRACY PAUL
KYLE PEARSON
LAUREN PECK
KELLY PEDERSON
HAROLD PEETE
NELSON L PENA
ROSTIO PENERA
KENNETH PEOPLES
MANNY PEREZ
MARY ELIZABETH PEREZ
EMILY PEREZ
MICHAEL PEREZ
ERIK PERKINS
KATE PERKINS
NICHOLAS PERSHEY
TOM PERSKI

MARGARET PESQUERA
CATHY PETERS
SAM PETERS
TERI PETERSON
BECKY PETREIKIS
KIRSTEN PFEIFFER
TOM PHEE
JEREMY PHELAN
ALLISON PHELPS
BRYAN PHILLIPS
JAMES PIEHL
ED PIENTA
SUZANNE PIERCE-COGGINS
DAVID PILARCZYK
AMY PINGITORE
MARIANNE PIOCH
BRIAN PIROK
SUE PITKIN
KAREN PITTATSIS
ANNA PLACENTI
SCOTT PLACKO
TYRONE PLAZA
RICHARD PLEITT
DEANNA PODGORNY
AL PODGORSKI
LINDA POHLMAN
MIKE POLANEK
GRZEGORZ POLOWCZYK
DONNA POMEROY
PHYLLIS POMETTA
JOHN POMPE
PAUL PONTICELL
KATHY PONZIANO
NAOMI POPE
RISA POPELKA
MARC POPOVICI
JAMIE POPP
RON PORRAS
REBECCA POSING
KAREN POTEMPA
CANDACE POTEMPA
MARY ANN POTTER
MELVIN POWELL
TOM POWERS
CINDY POWERS
CHUCK PREEN
BEAU PREER
BETH PREIS
CHRIS PREUCEL
ERIN PRIMDAHL
JEN PROKOP
KEVIN PRUDENCIO
CHERYL PUGH
GREGG PUPECKI
L C PURINS
KELLY PYNE
GLENNA PYZIK
DANNY QUANSTROM

One of Capture My Chicago's most active groups:

West Suburban Chicago Flickrers

http://www.flickr.com/groups/wscf/

1,170 Photos
193,782 Votes

SAMUEL BARR
CATIE BARRON
BETH BROUSIL
MICHAEL BROWN
ALI CHINLUND
THERESA CRAMER
PHILIPP CRISOLOGO
JAN CRITES
MARICEL CRUZ
JUSTIN DEARE

ALLAN DELOS REYES
MANUEL DIAZ
DAMIAN DOCKERY
RICHARD DUSLACK
CHRIS GINGRICH
ART HILL
KERRI IZATT
LISA JARRETT
KELLY JOHNSON
CHERYL KELLY

SCOTT LEWIS
DAVID LEWIS
ADRIAN LOVATT
ERIK LYKINS
MARIA MACHIN
MARIA MALAYTER
ED MARSHALL
ERICA MARSHALL
HARKER MILEY
FRANCISCO MONTES

PHILLIP MOODY
KAREN NUZZO
JOE ORBAN
LAURA ROWAN
ANDREA SAHS
JUNE STILL-FLORES
JOYCE STUTIKA
ALLEN TUNGET

BRETT R	KEVIN ROCIO	PAM SALEY	OKSANA SHANLEY	PATTY SIMPSON	J. STERLING SMITH	CHRIS STAMM	GEORGE STRUMPF	MARY THORNE	BLANCA VELEZ
KEITH RACHUBINSKI	JAVIER ROD	AURORA SAMAR	CRYSTAL SHARP	INDIA SIMPSON	KATHERINE SMITH	JOSEPH STANFORD	RAY STUBNER	MICHELLE THORNTON	KAREN VENA
SCOTT RADLIFF	RON RODEN	JAVIER SAN MIGUEL	DOUGLAS SHARP	JERRY SIMS	SHANYA SMITH	JUDITH STANISLOVAITIS	KATHRYN SUBJECT	JULIE THORNTON	JASMINKA VENETI
ELIZABETH RADTKE	LYNN RODIE	ABEL SANCHEZ	CARI SHEEHAN	ERNEST SIMS	ANGELA SMITH	DIANE STANKAVICH	KATE SUCHOLL	DEAN THORSEN	HEIDI VIENUP
JON RADTKE	JOSUE RODRIGUEZ	GERARDO SANCHEZ	MARILYN SHELBY	PATRICIA SINGER	ABIGAIL SMITH	BRANDON STANTON	JEFF SUDDETH	KIMBERLEY THUNHERST	JOSE VILLARREAL
DAN RADTKE	RUBY RODRIGUEZ	KIRK SANCHEZ	DENISE SHELTON	JANET SINIBALDI	RONNIE JO SOKOL	JOHN STAUFFER	JAMIE SULIT	CHRIS TOFANO	NICOLE VITALE
PATTI RAIMAN	FEDERICO RODRIGUEZ	LEE ANN SANDERSON	PEGGY SUE SHEPHERD	JANE SIZEMORE	JESSICA SOKOLOWSKI	KENNETH STEELE	MOLLIE SULLIVAN	GEORG TOFT	DAWN VITALONE
YASMIN RAMMOHAN	EVELYN RODRIGUEZ	NIKKI SANTOS	JASON SHEPUTIS	BRADLEY SKOF	JOSEPH SOLT	LEONIDAS STEFANOS	PAM SULLIVAN	MELISSA TOMASEWSKI	KATHY VONDRACEK
LINDA RAMOS	MARCIE ROGERS	KRYSTAL SANTOS	DAN SHEPUTIS	CRAIG SKORBURG	SANDY SOMERMAN	LINDA STEGER	RYAN SULLIVAN	PHILIP TOMHAVE	ROBIN VORREITER
BRIAN RANGEL	ANNE ROGERS	NORM SANTOS	GREG SHERGOLD	MARCIA SKWAREK	MARILYN SOMMER	MICHAEL STEINBERG	SHERY SULLIVAN	ROBERT TOON	JAMES VOVES
HEATHER RASCHKE	CARL ROLLBERG	RICK SANZ	LAURA SHERIDAN	JOHN F SKWAREK JR	KENNY SOMMER	FRED STEINKEN	WILLIAM SULLIVAN	META ROSE TORCHIA	MADHUR VYAS
BOB RATHELL	GINO ROMOZZI	SPENCER SANZ					ANN SULLIVAN	MARTIN TORRES	RASA R
KEN RATHJE	CARL RONSCHKE	CHRIS SAQUIDO					CAROLINE SULLIVAN	MARILYN TOURNIER	SAM W
DAVE RAUBE	PEDRO ROSA	CATHLIN SASO					TOM SUMMERS	MIKE TOWERS	JAMIE W
MARGO RAUBE	JIM ROSANDER	BETH SASSO					MEGAN SUMMERS	BRAD TOWNSEND	SCOTT W
DINESH RAVEENDRAN	MIKE ROSATI	RICHARD SAUER	**One of Capture My Chicago's most active groups:**				BILL SUNDAY	GREG TRACEY	CHASE W
GERARDO RAVELO	GLENN ROSE	GORDON SAUER	**Chicago PhotoCOOP**				T SURFACE	CAMILLE TRAFICANTO	DIANNE WADDELL
B K RAY	DEBBIE ROSE	JOANN SCALPONE	http://www.photocoop.org				MARTIN SURGES	AARON TRAVIS	ANNE WAGNER
VIDEO RAY	MARLENE ROSECRANS	ELIZABETH SCHAAF					PAUL & PHYLLIS SURPRENANT	TERRY TRIBBLE	CORRIE WAHOUT
HALLIE REDMAN	SARAH ROSECRANS	JOEY SCHAEFFER	**1,294 Photos**					KIM TRIUNFOL	COLLEEN WALDOCH
RON REECE SR	LIES ROSEMA	LARRY SCHAIBLEY	**93,597 Votes**				RACHEL SUSIO	PHYLLIS TRODDEN	RICHARD WALENDA
ELIZABETH REESE	ALEXANDRE ROSEN	SANDRA SCHEETZ-WISE					LARRY SUTHERLAND	ALLAN TRUEBLOOD	JANELLE WALKER
NATHAN REEVES	LYNN ROSSELL	KEVIN SCHEY					TAMMY SUTPHIN	MAGGIE TRUNDA	CHRISTIAN WALKER
MELISSA REGAN	ANDREW ROSSETTI	KALLEY SCHILLEN					DANEL SVALENKA	DAVID TRYBAN	BURNHAM WALLACE
AARON REID	VICKI ROSSING	CATHERINE SCHLESINGER					ARIC SWANEY	AMY TSCHIDA	TONY WALLACE
SAMUEL REIMAN	EDWIN ROTH	CHRIS SCHMAL	STEVEN A. RICHARDS	SUZANNE GIANDONATO	ANITA LAMBERT	DANA SERLING	JV SWANSON	OLGA TSVYNTARNA	GERALD WALLACE
ALI REIN	DAVE ROTH	RICHARD SCHMIDT	DANIEL BARTEL	HUGO GONZALEZ	DANIEL LANDSTROM	MALLORY TAGLIA	MEAGAN SWATEK	KATIE TUMAVICH	BURNHAM WALLACE
JOSI REIN	MYLES ROTHSTEIN	BARBARA SCHMIDT	KRISTEN CASTON	SETH GUTING	ROBIN MAHER	SHERYL THOMAS	GLYN SWEETS	CHRISTOPHER TUSCAN	LINDA WALLACE
RUTH REISE	DOMINIC ROTONDO	KRISTINA SCHMITT	SHERYL CHAPMAN VRHEL	GURLEY HARDIN	GEORGE MALAMIS	DAVID THOMAS	ALAN SWIATEK	KYLE TWENTY	ALEX WALLS
RENEE RENDLER-KAPLAN	ANDY ROUSEY	JACOB SCHNELL	JOHN CROUCH	JOHN HARRISON	EDWARD MEEHAN	BOB VALLANDINGHAM	BOB SWININOGA	BILL TYGIELSKI	ELIZABETH WALLS
JOHN RENFROW	DAVID J. ROWBERRY	MARY BETH SCHOLTES	CAROLYN DIMMICK	CARLOS JIMENEZ	LESLIE MURRAY	STEVE YOUNG	ANTOINETTE SYKES	TERRI TYLER	CHARLES WALNECK
FRANK RENNHAK	JANET ROWE	STEVEN SCHROEDER	CARA FRISON	GINA JOZAITIS	SUSAN PHILLIPS	RACHEL ZANDER	WAYNE SZARA SR.	CLAIRE UNDERWOOD	MARGARET WALSH
STEVE RETZ	JACLYN ROWE	CINDY SCHUCH		AMANDA KEEGAN	RON PORRAS		AL SZOPINSKI	ADRIAN UNDERWOOD	MANERVIA WALTON NEWMAN
KATHY REYES	PAUL ROWE	DEBRA SCHUERR					JILL SZPONDER	MARGARET UNGER	SHEILA WANTIEZ
LINDA REYES	JOHN RUBERRY	ANNESSA SCHULTZ					SCOTT SZYBOWICZ	CRAIG URBAN	MICHAEL WARD
MICHAEL REYES	DAVE RUBINI	TOM SCHULTZ					MALLORY TAGLIA	MARLA URBANEK	TIM WARD
LISA RICHARDSON	JIM RUFFATTO	DONNA SCHULZE					ROBERT TAMBURELLO	GABRIEL V	ROSEMARY WARNER
LAURA RICKS	BARBARA RUPPERT	LINDA SCHUMACHER					BOB TANNER	THOMAS VACLAVEK	KATHLEEN WARNER
MICHELLE RIECHERS	BARBARA RUSS	NANCY SCHUNEMAN					FAIGIE TANNER	BRUNO VAIS	BRITNEY WARREN
CLAUDE RIENDEAU	MARVIN RUSSELL	STEVEN SCHWAB					NIMA TARADJI	PATTI VALDEZ	ASHER WARSO
ALVIN RIESBECK	ANGELINA RUSSO	CANDICE SCHWAKE					BEN TARVER	KATIE VALENTINO	DAVID WATERS
GIULIANA RIGALI	ROBERT RUTHERFORD	SARAH SCHWARTING					SEAN TAYLOR	CARRIE VALENTINO	TOM WATKINS
ERICA RINDE	CINDY RUTZ	JENNI SCIACCA					LARRY THOMAS	AMADOR VALENZUELA	TYRONE WATSON
RICK RINGLE	KATIE RYAN	SANDY SCOTT					GEORGE THOMAS	JACK VALIN	WESLEY WATSON
RAYMOND RIOS	JEANNE RYAN	DONNA SCOTT					JOHN THOMAS	DEBORAH VAN DER HARST	KATHY WAWAK
CATHY RISKE	BILL RYERSON	MAXINE SCOTTY					PETER THOMAS	HARRY VAN DYKE	FLO WAWCZAK
HENRY RISTIC	HOPE RYMARZ	KAREN SEAHOLM					MARLO THOMAS	TAMMY VAN SLEE	LILIANNA WAWRZYNIAK
JEFF RIZNER	LYNN SABIA	CHUCK SEBASTIAN					MARIAMMA THOMAS	JOSEPH VANERIO III	ALTON WEATHERSPOON
LESLIE ROACH	SARAVANAN SADASIVAM	JACKIE SEBASTIAN					DAVID THOMAS	BARBARA VANHAL	DAVID WEBSTER
D ROB	DAVID SAENZ	SARAH SEELEY					GERALD THOMAS	PAT VANKIRK	CHRISTINA WEGLOSKI
TOM ROBAK	RICK SAGAN	ALAN SEIDL					SHERYL THOMAS	STEVE VARACALLI	CLAUDE WEGLOSKI
CHRISTOPHER ROBBIN	MIKE SAGE	CATHRYN SEITZ					TYVOANGA THOMAS	BERENICE VARELA	WALTER WEGLOSKI
GEORGE ROBERTS	KAREN SAJEWSKI	C SELSOR					AMANDA THOMAS	ALGIS VASONIS	PAUL WEGLOSKI
HARLEY ROBERTS	HANK SAJOVIC	SARAH SERBINSKI					VICTORIA THOMPSON	JUDY VAUGHN	ALICE SUE WEGLOSKI
DREW ROBERTSON	DAWN SAKARZYNSKI	FRANK SESKO					BILL THOMPSON	GREG VAUGHN	CHRISTINE WEHRLE
PAUL ROBINSON	GEORGE SALEK	MEERA SETHI					SCOTT THOMPSON	KATHRYN VEATH	MICHAEL WEILAND
MAMIE ROBINSON	FADI SALEM	MIMOSA SHAH					BRITTANY THOMPSON	GRACIELA VEGA	ARLENE WEIRICH
JEROME ROCHELLE	STEVE SALERNO	JOHN SHANKLAND					CHRIS THOMPSON	JOSE VELEZ	
			CHARLES SHERWIN	VINCENT SLOWIAK	JOHN SORRENTINO	RICHARD STELMASZEK			
			CHRISTOPHER SHEVCHIK	ROY SLOWINSKI	RAFAEL SOSA	PETE STENBORG			
			RYCA SHIH	SCOTT SLUTSKY	JOEL SOTO	LISA STEPHENSON			
			BRUCE SHIPYOR	PREMYSL SMEJKAL	NANCY SOUCEK	SCOTT STEVENS			
			IAN SHORR	DON SMETZER	LOU SOUCEK	JEFF STEVENSON			
			KELLEY SHORR	KAREN SMILIE	HEIDI SOUTHARD	BREANNA STEWART			
			ROSS SHRESTHA	JEAN SMILINGCOYOTE	ROBIN ANN SOWIZROL	JUNE STILL-FLORES			
			WENDY SHULIK	SALEAH SMITH	SHARON SPAKAUSKY	MICHAEL STINEMAN			
			LEE SHULTZ	TONY SMITH	TOM SPARKS	RENEE STOCK			
			JOEL SIBICK	PATTY SMITH	AMI SPENCER	GREGG STOCKEY			
			ANDREW SIEDELMANN	LINDSEY SMITH	CHRISTIE SPERRY	LEE STRAHLER			
			BRIAN SIEGEL	BRITTANY SMITH	CHARLENE SPIKES	SILVIU STRAIN			
			KAREN SIERGEY	VICKI SMITH	ERIC SPIVEY	JENNIFER STRAKA			
			JUSTICE SIERRA	LUCY SMITH	REGINA SPRINGER	DESTINY STREET			
			LINDSEY SIKULA	MELISSA SMITH	CHRISTINE SROKA	DIANE STREICHER			
			DONALD SILBERMAN	KAREN SMITH	MEAGEN ST. LOUIS	RON STREIT			
			BARBARA SILBERT	JEREMY SMITH	RONALD STAGG	LARRY STRICKLAND			
			MARK SILZELL	ZACHARY SMITH	JOHN STAHL	JAKE STRINGER			
			CHRISTINE SIMONS	BRENDA SMITH	ROBERT STALLWORTH	DIANE STROTHERS			

HOWARD WEISBART	MARISSA WELSH	MARION WHITE	WILLIAM WILKINS	FC WILLIAMSON	KATHLEEN WOLF	ROLAND WOZNIAK	BOBBY XHILONE	STEVE YOUNG	REBECCA ZELDENRUST
CAROLYN WEISS	TAMMY WENDT	JILL WHITE	MIKE WILKINS	KEVIN WILSON	BOB WOLF	BRUCE WRENN	DOCK YANCEY	CHARLES YOUNG	KELLY ZENG
LAURA WEISS LYNGAAS	MICKEY WENDT	GINGER WHITE	JEFF WILLARD	THERESE WILSON	SHARI WOLFE	RACHEL WRIGHT	TODD YATES	LARRY YOUNGBERG	YANYAN ZHANG
IAN WEIVODA	KELLY WENZEL	CAROL WHITE	JOSEPH WILLERTH	MICHAEL WILSON	CHRISTINE WOLFF	MATTHEW WRIGHT	GLENN YEAGER	TOMMY Z	REGINA ZIEMANN
MITCHELL WELKA	KRISTIN WERLER	PAT WHITNEY	CRESANDRA WILLIAMS	JORDAN WILSON	MARLA WOLFINGER	ROBERT WROBEL	BRETT YEPEZ-O'BOYLE	ALISSA ZABEL	ANTOINETTE ZIEMNIAK
JENNIFER WELLINK	KATELYNN WERRBACH	JUDY WIEGAND	BETH WILLIAMS	STEPHANIE WINSTON	RHONDA WSOL-HOZZIAN	JOHN WOLINSKI	CHRISTOPHER YETTER	ASHLEY ZAKAR	DON ZOCHOWSKI
DENISE WELLS	STEVE WEST	ANDREA WIESE	JOSHUA WILLIAMS	AGNIESZKA WIOSNA	RAMONA WOOD	CARL WU	FRANCES YORK	SEBASTIAN ZANGARA	LAURA ZOMBORACZ
JANUARY WELSH	JOHN WETZEL	ERICK WILCZYNSKI	CANDACE WILLIAMS	RICHARD WITKIEWICZ	LYLE WOODRUM	LORI WYATT	KALI YOST	JOY ZAVALA	EMELIA ZUCCHERI
RONDA WELSH	LAURA WHALEN	KRISTA WILDER	LISA WILLIAMS	RICHARD WOLDMAN	JENNIFER WOOLLEY	ELLIE WYDEVEN	KATHLEEN YOUNG	AGNES ZAWADZKA	
SHANE WELSH	TIFFANY WHISLER	LAUREN WILKINS	JANINE WILLIAMSON	TRISH WOLF	KATHERINE WYER	LIZ WORTH	JOHN YOUNG	ILENE ZEIGER	

If you like what you see in the book and on the companion DVD, be sure to check out these photographers' Web sites. A few even sell prints so you may be able to snag your favorite photos from the project to hang on your wall.

STEVEN A. RICHARDS — ArtPhotoChicago.com
PAULA ABBOTT — magickwillow.com
JODI ADAMS — jodiadams.net
SAM ADAMS — samueladamsphoto.com
MAREK AKSAMIT — mareksphotography.com
NAKEYISHA AISHA AL-HALEEM — blurosepixels.webs.com
TONY ALBERTI — flickr.com/photos/talberti/
NICK ALECK — nickaleck.smugmug.com
ANDRE ALFORQUE — alforque.com
MIKE ALLEE — flickr.com/photos/mikeallee
JON ALLEGRETTO — jartistry.com
NICK ALLEN — flickr.com/photos/nickallen
ANTHONY ALTAMORE — anthphotography.com
IGNACIO ALVAREZ — trumancollege.edu/~photography/
CARRIE ANDERSON — flickr.com/khakiaraki
SETH ANDERSON — b12partners.net/wp/
KATHIE ANDERSON — kathieandersonllc.smugmug.com/
B. ANDRÁS — Flickr.com/BADigiFoto/Collections
ADELLE ANG — flickr.com/photos/angadellepatricia/
KEVIN APGAR — kapgar.com
DAVID APRIL — soasoas.com
ERWIN ARAOS — flickr.com/photos/fatalysis/

ARACELI ARROYO — chicagophotos.blogspot.com
SHAY ATKINSON — facebook.com/fotochez
DWIGHT AVENT — aventprinting.com/photo.html
LIZ AVERY — capturecincinnati.com/people/SmilingZil
JOE BABULA — joebabula.wordpress.com/
GREG BAILEY — GregabyteGraphics.com
ASHLEY BAILEY — ashleybaileyphotography.com
DAVE BAIOCCHI — studiobaiocchi.com
MIKE BAKER — betterphoto.com/?3rdeye
MARK BALDWIN — flickr.com/photos/9570987@N04/
JOE BALYNAS — flickr.com/photos/muledriver/
JAMES BANKS — flickr.com/photos/glow_worm/
TOMMY BARBEE — fuzzythoughts.wordpress.com/
ANDREW BARICKMAN — ajbarickman.com
KIM BARKEY — kimbarkey.com
ROBERT BARNES — rjbarnesphoto.com
SAMUEL BARR — samuelbarr.com
DANIEL BARTEL — danielbartel.com
TAMARA BELL — tamarabellphotography.com/blog/
MARGE BELLISARIO — forestviewlounge.com
ELLEN BELLUOMINI — ellenbelluomini.com
FRANK BENDA — flickr.com/frankbenda

MICHAEL BENNETT — flickr.com/photos/michaelbennett
APRIL BERN — flickr.com/photos/rottnapples/
DEAN BERNAL — decoratewithart.net
AMY BESTHOFF — jeffsautoservicelith.com
LEE BEY — leebey.com
KATHY BIAGI — flickr.com/photos/26160580@N07/popular-interesting/
TOM BLAKELY — ttbphotographic.com
JOHN BLANTON — johnhblantonphotos.ifp3.com
HAROLD BLUM — flickr.com/photos/hbchicago/sets/72157616181972039/
DUSTY BODRERO — flickr.com/photos/dustybodrero/
WILLIAM BORN — wborndds.com
LILLY BOUZIDE — becomebeauty.net/Lilly
MICHAEL BRACEY — mjbphotography.com
LEATHEIA BRADY RHODES — almit.ifp3.com
TERI BRIESKE — myspace.com/45901182
MAUREEN BRILL — myspace.com/artisticbrew
SVEN BROGREN — sven-brogren.fineartamerica.com/
DIANE BRONSTEIN — DianePatricia.com
BETH BROUSIL — flickr.com/photos/beth_b75/
JOHN BROWN — sites.google.com/site/cerealfun/
MICHAEL BROWN — zhibit.org/mickeybphotography

AARON BROWN — aaronbrownphotos.com
CATHERINE BROWN — valpovelvet.com
KATHLEEN BUHRMANN — ksbphoto.wordpress.com
JANESSA BULLEN — janessabullen.com
MINDY BUSH — 3-cubed.com
DANIEL BUTLER — danielbutler.daportfolio.com/
ADAM BYKOWSKI — redbubble.com/people/Bykowski
EDWARD CALDERON — ECALDERONPHOTOGRAPHY.COM
J. CHRIS CALLAHAN — JChrisCallahan.com
BRIAN CALLAHAN — flickr.com/photos/shinsanbc/
DAVE CAMERON — flickr.com/photos/normalityrelief/
NICOLE CAMPBELL — flickr.com/photos/heirophantress
AL CANCEL — secretgardeninc.com
ANTHONY CARDOZA — acpainter824.com
JASON CARREL — facebook.com/jasoncarrel
JOHN CARUSO — carusophotos.com/
SAMMY CASSIN — MILESTONESPHOTOS.COM
ANTONIO (TONY) CASTILLO — tonycastillo.net
KRISTEN CASTON — kristencaston.com
BILL CERMAK — billcermakphotos.shutterfly.com/
ROLANDO CERVANTES — flickriver.com/photos/rolandin
SHERYL CHAPMAN VRHEL — sherylchapmanphotography.com
KASHIF CHATMON — moband.blip.tv
GREG CHERNIET — flickr.com/photos/greg-cherniet
JOHN CHIMON — flickr.com/photos/12243177@N05/
TRACI CHIRILLO — LBOriginal.com

CHUNSUM CHOI — chunsum.com
MAUREEN CLANCY, SSND — pathtorelaxation.com
JULIA CLARK — flickr.com/juliaclark42
SANTA CLAUS — SantaChicago.com
TRAVIS CLEMENT — travisclement.com
JEREMY CLIFF — flickr.com/jeremycliff
MATTHEW COGLIANESE — cogs8.deviantart.com
MIKE COLEMAN — flickr.com/photos/zhaonameloc
APRIL COLLINS — CNCcreativePix.com
BRYAN COUSINEAU — flickr.com/photos/bryansimages
ERIC CRAIG — ericcraigstudios.com
THERESA CRAMER — flickr.com/photos/keleka656/
GARY CRAWFORD — NegroLeagueLegends.org
LARRY CRIDER — printroom.com/pro/larrycriderphotography
PHILIPP CRISOLOGO — flickr.com/photos/pcrisologo/
BRIAN CRISSIE — briancrissie.smugmug.com
JAN CRITES — flickr.com/photos/janny4jc/
JOHN CROUCH — flickr.com/crouch
MARICEL CRUZ — maricelcruz.com
KATHRYN CUNNINGHAM — atravelersview.org
CATHLEEN DAUM — cjdcathyd.webs.com/
RYAN DAVIS — ryandavisphotography.com
JESSICA DAVIS — flickr.com/photos/jdavisphoto/
TRACY DEIS — tldphoto.com
ALLAN DELOS REYES — flickriver.com/photos/24109237@N05
KEN DERRY — KenDerry.com

MANUEL DIAZ — flickr.com/photos/myn91/
MELANIE DIAZ — flickr.com/photos/melvdiaz/sets/
SAM DICKEY — flickr.com/photos/akagoldfish
JENNIFER DICKSON — dicksonart.net
CAROLYN DIMMICK — myspace.com/throughthecameralenz
PETE DOHERTY — dohertyimages.com
STEPHEN DOKOUPIL — lightzone.deviantart.com/
JIM DOMIANO — chicagosnaps.com
BRIAN DRABIK — flickr.com/photos/35261410@N00/
GARY DUBOFSKY — flickr.com/photos/duboman
ELAINE EIGER — elaineeiger.com
ISRA EKBAL — snowcityarts.com
DAVID ELLIS — flickr.com/daveyisnotaphotographer
PEGGY ENQUIST — picasaweb.google.com/penquist/StarredPhotos#
PATRICIA EPPS — photo.net/photos/pattography
SCOTT EVANS — scottevansphoto.com
KEVIN FAGAN — kev-kfactory.blogspot.com/
GEOFF FAULKNER — geofffaulkner.com
EUGENE FELIX — eugenefelix.com
CHRIS FENISON — chrisfenison.com
TOM FENNELL — flickr.com/TEFennell4
JOHN FINNEGAN — finnegankoppgallery.com
ED FISHER — flickr.com/photos/ehfisher/
CHRISTINE FITZPATRICK — truenorthphotography.com
THERESE FLANAGAN — thereseflanagan.com
ARCHIE FLORCRUZ — whateverland.com

LORENZO FLORIAN — flickr.com/people/30887229@N05/
MARTIN FLUCH — flickr.com/photos/mfluch/
LARRY FOSSE — larryfosse.photopoints.com
STEVE FRANGELLA — stevefrangella.com
KAY FREDERICK — flickr.com/photos/sparkyluck/sets/
MICHAEL FRIEDBERG — michaelfriedbergphotography.com
CARA FRISON — carafrison.com
ODED FROMOVITZ — odedfr.photolight.co.il
WILLIAM FULTZ II — flickr.com/photos/31024064@N05/
SHARON GAIETTO — sharongaiettophotography.shutterfly.com
JAMES GALEN — volleyphotos.shutterfly.com
GREG GALLAGHER — greggallagher.com
SEAN GALLAGHER — iqretouching.com
ABHI GANJU — chicagofineartphotography.com
CHRIS GANS — chrisgans.com
MICHELLE GANTNER — flickr.com/loonachic
MAXINET GARCIA — mtphotologue.carbonmade.com
ROLOUR GARCIA — claudinegarcia.com
KIMBERLY GATES — kgates.zenfolio.com
JORGE GERA — jorgegeraphotography.com
JEFF GEREW — C7Photo.com
DAVID GIBSON — davegibsonphoto.com
MARIE GILBERT — MarieGilbertDesign.com
TOM GILL — lapstrake.blogspot.com/
PAT GLEASON — patgleason.com
ADAM GNOTH — flickr.com/adamgnoth

JODI GOLDSTEIN
jodiellen.com

LORNE GOLMAN
youtube.com/user/perfectcutproduction

GERARD GOUSMAN
chopfire.blogspot.com/

W VALLEN GRAHAM
wvallen.com

JOHN GREDE
john-grede-photos.com

TAMMY GREEN
tammygreen.com

JUSTIN GREEN
flickr.com/photos/justingreen19

GOING GREEN
gg2137.com

WADE GRIFFITH
wadegriffith.net

SARAH GROSS
sarahgrossphotography.com

GABRIELA GUILLERMO-GARZA
flickr.com/people/coopersvictim87/

KRISTINA GURNEY
KGphotodesign.com

SUZANNE HAEGELE
flickr.com/photos/suzanneimagination/

NATALIE HAGEN
flickr.com/photos/warrior_poet/

BRIAN HAGY
brianhagy.com

DAVID HAILS
davehailsdigitalimages.com/

GEOFF HALLIDAY
halliday.smugmug.com

BILL HANNIGAN
THREEMENINKILTS.COM

GURLEY HARDIN
flickr.com/photos/the_light_catcher/

CHRIS HARGREAVES
iCanCyou.com

KEITH HARRIS
khcphotographics.com

JOHN HARRISON
jnhphoto.redbubble.com/

HEATHER HARTY
heatherhartyphotography.webs.com

RICH HARVEY
richeeyreflections.ifp3.com

RALPH HASELTINE
haseltine-photo.com

IAN HASELTINE
haseltine-photo.com

JEN HATZ
autumntree.com

KIMBERLY HAUMAN
kimhaumanphotography.com

RICK HAUSER
relocationadvisorsgroup.com

TIM HEAD
headphotography.com

AMANDA HEIN
amandahein.com

MARIA HENAO
flickr.com/cammicams

CLIFTON HENRI
cliftonhenri.com

MAURA HERNANDEZ
maurahernandez.com

JESSICA HERNANDEZ
iliedtotheangel.deviantart.com/

BECCA HEUER
beccaheuer.com

ANDREW HICKEY
flickr.com/photos/shookiemookie

SHARON HICKS-BARTLETT
sojournerrides.blogspot.com

ART HILL
windycityart.com

CALVIN HINSON
calvindamien.com

AMY HONNEY
afoxphoto.com

STEPHAN HOOG
sjhphoto.zenfolio.com/

SUSAN HOOPER
performforthelove.com/.

BOB HORSCH
horschgallery.com

LINDA HORTON
lindahortonphotography.com

JIM HORTON
jimojimo.smugmug.com

TOM HYLAND
tomhylandphotography.com

IRFAN IBRAHIM
flickr.com/photos/30685050@N05/

KEN ILIO
flickr.com/photos/kenilio

JULIE IVENS
flickr.com/photos/julieivens/

MARY IVORY
maryivory.com

KERRI IZATT
flickr.com/photos/kerriphotog/

GARY JACKSON
firewhenreadypottery.com

JENNIFER JACKSON
jenniferjackson.artspan.com

KIP JACOBS
krazygrain.com

DIANA JACOBSON
jalynphotography.com

CHUCK JANDA
chuckphotospot.com

LISA JARRETT
twitter.com/lisaannjarrett

ALAA JAWAD
flickr.com/photos/26654815@N08/

JOACHIM JOCSON
facebook.com/joenavy24

NIKKI JOHNSON
flickr.com/photos/8977254@N08/

LYNDON JOHNSON
flickr.com/photos/ljsphotos

ALLEN JOHNSON
sirallen.tumblr.com

KELLY JOHNSON
kellyjohnsonphotography.com

JEFFERY C. JOHNSON
flickr.com/photos/jefferycjohnson

JONATHAN MICHAEL JOHNSON
planckstudios.com

JIM JONES
flickr.com/photos/jtj3/

ADAM JOSEPH
adamjoe.com

GINA JOZAITIS
flickr.com/gina4xoxoxo

LORENA JURADO
flickr.com/photos/lorena_every-passing-moment/

DAVID KAUFMAN
linkedin.com/in/davidmkaufman

CHERYL KELLY
flickr.com/photos/cher12861/

JOHN KELLY
nocoastpunk.deviantart.com/

TARAS KHLIBOVYCH
phototerry.net/

EDWARD KIMBOWA
edphoto.imagekind.com

MARK KIME
Valpomall.com

TIM KING
flickr.com/photos/timo3k

MARK KINSMAN
flickr.com/photos/mbkinsman/

PETER KOCH
photographybypeterjkoch.com

DESIREE KOH
desireekoh.com

CURTIS KOJO-MORROW
mysankofa.shutterbugstorefront.com/g/

THOMAS KOST
flickr.com/photos/toast322/

NICOLE KOURTIS
flickr.com/photos/nicolekourtis

ELENA KOVALEVICH
flickr.com/photos/ekovalev

MARCIN KOZLOWSKI
photoshop.com/user/kozlmar

KURT KRAMER
flickr.com/photos/havanai/

MIRIAM KRAVIS
miramsphotos.com

JOE KULYS
joekulys.com

KEVIN KUPHAL
flickr.com/photos/oblik

JEAN LACHAT
jeanlachatphotography.com

JEROME LACROIX
pbase.com/lacroix

AMANDA LAKE
amandamichellelake.smugmug.com/

ANITA LAMBERT
flickr.com/photos/17958185@N04/

DANIEL LANDSTROM
flickr.com/photos/dlandstrom/

JOHN LANGFELD
langfeldpoetry.blogspot.com

KEITH LANGOSCH
redbubble.com/people/klango90

BRENDAN LEAHY
flickr.com/photos/chirisheyes

ARTHUR LEE
flickr.com/photos/epyon

ERICA MARSHALL
muddyboots.org

STEPHANIE LEE
flickr.com/photos/buttermellow

FERDINAND MARTIJA
flickr.com/photos/ferdsfotos/

CHRISTIAN LEGAN
flickr.com/photos/christiaan_25/

CHERYL LEMANSKI
meryddianphotography.com/

GIGI LEONARD
gigileonard.etsy.com

SCOTT LEWIS
flickr.com/photos/kupfer29/

JEFF LEWIS
chicagophotoshop.com

JASON LEWIS
chicagophotoshop.com

BERT LIBOON
filamatibapa.spaces.live.com

HALEY LICATA
stateofhaley.blogspot.com

OLIVIA LIDDELL
olivialiddell.com

THERESA LIGGINS
theresaliggins.com

DWANE LINDSEY
drlphotographs.printroom.com

JODY LIU
flickr.com/j-exposures

ROY LOBENHOFER
lobenhofer.com/photography.htm

CONSTANCE B. LOFTIS
loftisphotographic.com

RICKEY LOGGINS
flickr.com/photos/riqqilin

TONIA LORENZ
stripedtigergraphics.com

ADRIAN LOVATT
flickr.com/photos/-adel-/

JULITA LUCAS
JulitaPhoto.com

JAY LUEBKING
jamminjay.com

ERIK LYKINS
flickr.com/photos/erik707

MARY MACIEJEWSKI
myspace.com/deartheo

JOHN MAGRUDER
flickr.com/photos/quantumjedi

MARK MAHAR
markmahar.ifp3.com

MARIA MALAYTER
docmaria.com

ROBERT MALDONADO
facebook.com/djahmahnee

MARYELLEN MALINOWSKI
infraredlight.com

JOHN MALOOF
johnmaloof.photoposts.org/

CINDY MAMMOSER
flickr.com/photos/kctwinmommy/

HECTOR MANDEL
dzphotovideo.com

ALBERTO MARCH-TOBELLA
grafmarc.com

MEGAN MARCINKUS
dOrktastik.deviantart.com/

AMANDA MARQUEZ
amandamarquez.com/photos

ED MARSHALL
esm.logic.net/

TORI LYNN MARTIN
torilynnphotography.com

JOHN MASTALERZ
smugmug.com/gallery/8072384_mnY7k/1/526227039_eWeUB

JILL MATSUHIRO
flickr.com/jnoriko

NATHAN MAYBERRY
nhmphoto.com

DAVID MAYHEW
davidmayhewphotography.com/

STEPH MAZANOWSKI
showmymoment.com

ARTHUR MAZZARO
ajmstudio.web.officelive.com/default.aspx

SHAWN MCCLEAVY
petplusconcierge.com

TERI MCDERMOTT
TeriMcDermott.com

KENNETH MCFARLAND
flickr.com/photos/outsanityphotos/

MARGO MCINTYRE
margomcintyrephotocreations.com

KIRK MCMAHON
flickr.com/photos/43243304@N00/

AMY MCTEAGUE
mcteaguephotography.com

JOSHUA MEDCALF
joshuamedcalf.daportfolio.com

ARSENY MEDVEDEV
FoquesPhoto.com

MALLORY MEINEN
web.me.com/meinenm

MAURICIO MEJIA
yesterdayslife.com/photofront/MauricioMejia

ELIZABETH MELAS
elizabethmelasphotography.com

ARMANDO MENDOZA
flickr.com/photos/hey_mando/

MICHAEL MESKIS
michaelmeskis.com/

DANIEL MESSICK
flickr.com/photos/daniel_g_messick_photography/

VERTA MIDCALF
freewebs.com/vertamidcalf-com/index.htm

HARKER MILEY
flickr.com/photos/mike_miley/sets/72157607332690750/

KEVIN MILLER
kmillerphoto.com

ERIC MILLER
ericwmiller.zenfolio.com

J DAVID MOELLER
jdavidmoeller.googlepages.com/

FRANCISCO MONTES
flickr.com/photos/montesphotography/sets/

PHILLIP MOODY
flickr.com/photos/pmoo/

JAMES MOORHEAD
jamesphotostudio.com

MIKE MORELAND
facebook.com/SubGeniusJRBobDobbs

MICHAEL MORRIS
flickr.com/photos/ithink2

DERREK MORRIS
MYSPACE.COM/MUDDVILLEGULLYBOYZ

MEAGHAN MULCAHY
myspace.com/lmao_rawr_itz_megan

MARK MULLIS
mmullis.com

MARIA MUNNICH
happyfridaystuff.com

RICHARD MUNNICH
thekaraokezonechi.com

CHARLIE NAEBECK
charlienaebeck.com

MAUREEN NAVADOMSKIS
dailyfarrell.blogspot.com

ERIC NELSON
ikymagoo.deviantart.com/

JANICE NELSON
jdnphotos.wordpress.com

KIERAN NEVIN-LYNCH
redfishbluefish.net

MARTIN NIETO
martinnieto.net

BORYS NIEWIADOMSKI
flickr.com/photos/thebrandnewyear

DEBBIE NOVAK
photos.capturemychicago.com/upload/1251861577537/thumb.jpg

MICHAEL J. NYCHAY
flickr.com/photos/m_nychay

JOE O'GRADY
shutterfly.com/pro/jogrady/dscimages

THOMAS O'GRADY
gameplancreative.com

CANDACE OLANDER
kitchengypsy.net

JOE ORBAN
flickr.com/people/vidular/

SAMANTHA ORTIZ
myspace.com/munchie888

LINDA OTERO
capturemychicago.com/people/lotero57

WAYNE OWEN
flickr.com/photos/italnstalln/

ANNE P
flickr.com/photos/opacity

CHRISTOPHER PACUTKOWSKI
zgradis.com

BRETT PADGETT
padgettphotography.com

JOHN PARLI
johnparliphotography.com

DARLENE PEACOCK
DARZAM.com

LAURENCE PEARLMAN
flickr.com/photos/photos_by_laurence/sets/72157606133994641/

JOE PEARSON
piehousesix.com

TERESA PEEK
flickr.com/photos/grasshopper_teresa

CRAIG PERRY
kuhnewer.com

KURT PERSCHKE
redballproject.com

TONY PETERMAN
anthony-photo.com

SARAH PETERS
flickr.com/photos/sosarah/

DRAGAN PETROVIC
laminarwind.com

MATT PHILBIN
pjmatthewsimages.com

JEFF PHILLIPS
superwide.blogspot.com

SUSAN PHILLIPS
flickr.com/photos/suephi/

RYAN PIERATT
rpieratt.deviantart.com

MARIUSZ PIEROG
burningshoes.com

RYAN PIKKEL
flickr.com/photos/xoxoryan/

VALERIE PIOTROWSKI
redbubble.com/people/vchen?utm_source

JAKE POEHLS
jacobpoehls.com

CASSANDRA POZULP
cassiepozulpphotography.sharemyartwork.com/

LISA PRESLEY
lisapresleyphotography.com

CAREY PRIMEAU
careyprimeau.com

JENNIFER PRINCE
fencepostphotography.com

YAN PRITZKER
facebook.com/pritzkerphoto

KEITH PULFORD
keefereye.com

ROB PUTNAM
flickr.com/photos/pixeldrops

KRISTINE QUANDEE
sartech.fatcow.com

SPEED RACER
flickr.com/photos/22950176@N06/

D RAHIM
photosbyerahim.wordpress.com

BIANCA RAMIREZ
flickr.com/photos/biancaprime/

MICHAEL RANK
twobites.wordpress.com

JUSTIN REED
flickr.com/photos/jreedphoto

JAMIE REED
cikaga.deviantart.com/

JESSICA REILLY
flickr.com/photos/xbratx/sets/

MATT RELSTAB
mattrelstab.com

CRITTER RETTIRC
flickr.com/photos/critter

SARAH RHEE
sarah-ji.com/blog

LINWOOD RILEY
soundclick.com/LinwoodRiley

BARTH RILEY
flickr.com/photos/27480139@N05/

BETH RITCHASON
bethsportraits.blogspot.com

BRIAN ROBERTS
twitter.com/brazepromotions

MARCUS ROBINSON
streetballegends10.shutterfly.com

JONATHAN ROBSON
jonathanrobsonphotography.com

RUBIN ROCHE
delobbo.com

ASHLEY RODAWOLD
facebook.com/cassandra.watson2?ref=nf#/profile.php?id=1606742940&ref=profile

DENISE ROGERS
denise-rogers.webs.com/

KELLEIGH ROMBA
flickr.com/photos/thisworldisour
DENISE ROMITA
SymmetryPhoto.ifp3.com
BETTY LARK ROSS
bettylarkross.com
LAURA ROWAN
flickr.com/photos/rowrlm/
BILL RUSS
billruss.com
WILLIAM RUTING
fireworksconsulting.com
JESSICA RYNNING
jessicaleighphotography.us
ANDREA SAHS
flickr.com/photos/andreasimages/
JAMES SANGSTER
jsdigital.ifp3.com
PRASANNA SARASWATHI KRISHNAN
flickr.com/photos/praspics
MATTHEW SAVARD
900hp.com
JAMES SAVINO
acornbay.shutterfly.com/#
PAUL SCHARFF
PaulScharffPhotography.com
JAREDE SCHMETTERER
jarede.net
DOROTHY SCHMIDT
crochetkookie.blogspot.com
JOHN SCHROEDER
photoentropy.com

AVI SCHWAB
flickr.com/photos/froboy
SCOTT SCOTT
flickr.com/photos/thepackagedesigner/
KATIE SCULLY
sparrowlab.cc
ANDREW SECRIST
asecristphotography.com
DANA SERLING
danajsphotography.blogspot.com
NIM SHARON
nimsharon.com
LUIS SIERRA MONTEVERDE
luisierra.com
PATRICK SKOFF
skoffpaintings.com
CHRISTOPHER SMITH
flickr.com/photos/christophervsmith/
HELENE SMITH
etsy.com/shop.php?user_id=6843195
ANDREW SOMMERFELD
andrewsommerfeld.com
STEPHEN SOSTARIC
flickr.com/photos/fresnel10/
KENNETH SPENCER
brokecompsoul.blogspot.com/
MATHEW SPOLIN
automatt.com/
JOHN STEEL
myspace.com/songwriterjohnsteel
JAMES STEELE
jamestimothy.com

LEAH STEINBAUER
iam.colum.edu/students/leah.steinbauer
MICHAEL STERNOFF
limitlessdreams.tv
CHRIS STEVENS
cstevensphoto.net
ELIZABETH STOCK
foto-monologue.blogspot.com
RICHARD STOCKMAN
risphotography.com/
J STONE
myspace.com/jstonefotog
KELLY STOTMEISTER
inthedaylightks.blogspot.com
MATT STRATTON
mattstratton.com
GRANT STROMBECK
videotherwise.com
JOYCE STUTIKA
flickr.com/photos/jlstutika/
KARTHIK SUDHIR
karthiksudhir.com
LISA SULLIVAN
flickr.com/photos/deadbettysdiner
STEPHEN SUNDBERG
smanofsteel76.blogspot.com/
RADHIKA SURAPANENI
flickr.com/people/18204116@N02/
LORI SWERDLOW
finishedfinely.com
STEPHANIE SYLVESTER
capturemychicago.com/people/bom2skate

PETER TAMBRONI
petertambroni.com
TRACY TARASIUK
flickr.com/photos/tara_siuk/
DAMON TAYLOR
flickr.com/photos/ocean_of_stars/
FRED TEIFELD
fredteifeld.com
KYLE TELECHAN
cityeyesphoto.com
GENE TENNER
flickr.com/photos/genetenner/
RALPH THOMAS
thomphoto.bozent.com
JASON THOMPSON
jasonhasideas.com
CHRIS TORRES
ctorresphoto.com
JENNIFER TRAN
ladyjade7013.shutterfly.com/
ARDITH TRUMPY
cheekradish.blogspot.com/
TRACY TUCHOLSKI
flickr.com/photos/tracesofme
LARRY TUCKMAN
flickriver.com/photos/citytripod/popular-interesting/
ALLEN TUNGET
capturemychicago.com/groups/West%20Suburban%20Chicago%20Flickrers
CHRIS TYRE
christyre.com

MIKE UMBREIT
umbieart.com/
BENJIE URBINA
BenjieUrbina.com
GINA URSO
ginaphotography.com
BOB VALLANDINGHAM
vallsimages.com
CHRISTOPHER VAUGHN
chrisvaughn.vox.com
TAYLOR VELDMAN
flickr.com/photos/emd7602
DAN VERSON
versonphotography.com
ANDREW VICKERS
andrew-vickers.com
CATIE VIHLEN
catievihlen.com
SCHUBERT VILLANUEVA
flickr.com/photos/svillanueva79
KEVIN CLARK VISITACION
kcfolio.com
KELLY VRANESIC
kellyvranesic.com
THIENTHU VU
khoidiem.org/imagegallery/index.php
LEE WACH
facebook.com/home.php?#/pages/Chicago-IL/Gemini-3-Productions/125548152426?ref=ts
COREY WAGEHOFT
trueformstudios.com

BRAD WAGGONER
photo.net/photos/bwaggoner
CODY WARD
CodyWard.com/
MIKE WAROT
flickr.com/photos/--mike--/
JAMES WATKINS
flickr.com/photos/26592941@N02/
EVAN WATSON
EvanAlexDesign.com
JOHN WEAVER
public.fotki.com/jw3/
PETER WELDON
pbase.com/pweldon
JOSH WELLINGTON
flickr.com/photos/joshwellington/
MARY WELLS
flickr.com/photos/marywells/
JENNIFER WHEELER
chicagoeventphotographer.com
OWEN WHISENANT
Starfire-Studios.com
MATT WHITMIRE
chicagovibealive.com
ROBERT WHITNEY
flickr.com/photos/pentachoron/
JASON WIDNEY
jasonwidney.com
GAIL WILEY
gailwileydesigns.com
TOM WILLIAMSON
photos.tomwilliamson.co.uk/

KEVIN WILLIS
myspace.com/elclem
JOHN WILSON
flickr.com/photos/johns-art
CHRISTOPHER WILSON
flickr.com/photos/sempernovus/sets
FRED WINSTON
fredwinstons.blogspot.com
ROBERT WOJTOW
RDUBPhoto.com
SIMON WOLAK
soaphoto.com/simon1977
MAGGIE WOLFF
flickr.com/notmargaret
JONATHAN WOOD
jonathanwoodphotography.com
SHARA WRIGHT
facebook.com/home.php?ref=home#/pages/Round-Lake-Beach-IL/Shara-Wright-Photography/136951326064?ref=ts
WILLIAM ZAKAVEC
cowjazz.us
RACHEL ZANDER
RachelZanderPhotography.zenfolio
STEPHEN ZEPEDA
flickr.com/photos/irongambit/
EDDY ZGONINA
epzphotoart2go.com
MARIUSZ ZIELEZNY
martiger.com
RYAN ZOGHLIN
rfoto.com

Chapter Introduction Photographers

The many photographers listed below helped shape the introduction page of each chapter. Many thanks to these fine folks (listed in order of appearance from left to right, top to bottom):

Friendly Faces: David April, Carey Primeau, Cindy Mammoser, Benjamin Oliver, Tori Lynn Martin, Christopher Wilson, John Crouch, Tori Lynn Martin, Shanya Smith, Robin Maher, Nikki Johnson, David April, Marianne Fosnow, John Caruso, Christopher Wilson, Shanya Smith, Jodi Goldstein, Jake Poehls, John Crouch, Aaron Burke, Joshua Medcalf, Kate Berman, Samuel Barr, Seth Guting, Maricel Cruz, Jennifer Jackson, Clifton Henri, Christopher Wilson, Jean Lachat, Anne P, John Parli, John Caruso, John Parli, Jonathan Robson.

Sports Spirit: Critter Rettirc, J. Chris Callahan, Brian Crissie, John Crouch, John Crouch, Jennifer Prince, Kelly Pederson, John Crouch, Geoff Halliday, Duane Hanacek, Robert Whitney, Kurt Brzuszkiewicz, Geoff Halliday, Brendan Leahy, Rolando Cervantes, Cindy Mammoser, Mike Umbreit, Jill Whitc, Michael Bracey, Steven Schwab, Joe O'Grady, Mallory Meinen, C Selsor, Laurence Pearlman, Pat Gleason, J. Chris Callahan.

Arts, Culture & Food: Christopher Wilson, David April, Geoff Halliday, Gary Jackson, Manuel Diaz, Becca Heuer, Wendy Armington, Critter Rettirc, Elizabeth Schaaf, Samuel Barr, Ana Garcia, Wade Griffith, Cathy Lavarda, Jonathan Robson, Andrew Hickey, Matthew Savard, Mathew Spolin, Tom Gill, James Nowak, Jonathan Robson, Maricel Cruz, Samuel Barr, David April, Jennifer Dickson, Renee Stock, Julita Lucas, Nona Flores, Sheryl Thomas, Laurence Pearlman, Tori Lynn Martin.

Scapes of All Sorts: Allan Delos Reyes, J. Chris Callahan, Anil Gandhi, Craig Skorburg, David Mayhew, Jason Lewis, Luis Sierra Monteverde, John Caruso, Jan Critcs, Allicon Phelps, John Caruso, Carrie Anderson, Yan Pritzker, David Mayhew, Tori Lynn Martin, B. András, John Caruso, Ken Ilio, John Mastalerz, Ma Anderson, Jonathan Robson, Cindy Mammoser, Jonathan Michael Johnson, Mira Keyes, Scott Evans, Jessica Hernandez, Manuel Diaz, Mike Umbreit, Tori Lynn Martin, Becky Morrissey.

Newsworthy: Erwin Araos, Mike Baker, Ed Fisher, J. Chris Callahan, Manuel Diaz, Carey Primeau, Tatiana Koutchma, John Crouch, Sean Gallagher, John Harrison, Mike Umbreit, B. András, Jonathan Robson, Chuck Janda, James Sangster, Yan Pritzker, Ken Ilio, John Harrison, B. András, Mike Umbreit, Peter Weldon, Bill Sunday, Carey Primeau, Andre Alforque, Christopher Vaughn, Maricel Cruz, Helen Lindsey, Sam Dickey, Jamie Reed, James Sangster, Tori Lynn Martin.

Pets: Patrick O'Neil, Dave Baiocchi, Ryca Shih, Gurley Hardin, April Mok, Michael Bennett, Luis Sierra Monteverde, Gina Juzaitis, David Pilarczyk, Avi Schwab, Tamara Bell, Critter Rettirc, Heather Keigher, Kelly Johnson, David April, Marianne Fosnow, Gurley Hardin, Katie Grossart, Nohemi Alcala, John Harrison, Anne P, Scott Placko, Mike Umbreit, Heather Keigher, Bryan Cousineau, Helen Lindsey, Maria Malayter, Mike Umbreit, Jonathan Wood, Ryca Shih.

Landmarks & Architecture: Charles Young, Jonathan Robson, Jason Lewis, Michael J. Nychay, John Caruso, John Crouch, Christopher Wilson, Eric Craig, Christopher Vaughn, Erica Marshall, Daniel Bartel, Critter Rettirc, John Kelly, Sven Brogren, Gabriela Guillermo-Garza, Jonathan Robson, Chris Tyre, John Crouch, Eric Craig, John Crouch, David Mayhew, Christopher Wilson, John Crouch, Craig Skorburg, Jonathan Robson, Maricel Cruz, John Chimon, Ken Ilio.

Recreation & Celebreation: Abhi Ganju, John Balzer, Erica Marshall, Brendan Leahy, Araceli Arroyo, John Harrison, Wes Dorszewski, Craig Skorburg, Abhi Ganju, Elizabeth Kubis, Allen Tunget, Luis Sierra Monteverde, Erica Marshall, Jeremy Cliff, Ken Ilio, Kevin Miller, Jonathan Robson, Ken Ilio, Mike Baker, Justin Deare, Archie Florcruz, Abhi Ganju, Ross Januszyk, Robert Casey, Rosanne Miezio, Michael Bracey, Harold Blum.

CHICAGO, YOU'RE MY KIND OF TOWN. AND WE'RE YOUR KIND OF FURNITURE STORE.

Value City Furniture. Proud to be furnishing America's homes for over 60 years, bringing Chicagoland magnificent miles of savings and selection!

Don't be Chi…visit us online at **vcf.com**!

Value City Furniture®
We make quality furniture affordable™